# THE COMPLETE INSTANT VORTEX
# AIR FRYER COOKBOOK

# The Complete
# INSTANT VORTEX
# AIR FRYER
# Cookbook

## Fry, Bake, and More in Your Instant Pot Air Fryer

### Linda Larsen

**ROCKRIDGE
PRESS**

*I dedicate this book to my*
*wonderful husband, Doug,*
*who has always supported me.*
*And he's a great sous chef!*

# Contents

# Introduction

**The air fryer has become a remarkably popular appliance.** Who knew that about a dozen years ago, that little R2-D2–shaped fryer would change the way many of us cook? My cooking life has been transformed by the air fryer. I never deep-fry foods anymore. Why would I, when I can get practically the same results using this miraculous appliance? I remember struggling with vats of hot cooking oil whenever I wanted to make French fries, and deep-frying doughnuts and chicken tenders, worrying the whole time about doneness and safety. The oil would splatter. The possibility of an accident would always be in the back of my mind. Then I would wonder what in the world to do with the quarts of hot, used oil. No longer!

This is my seventh air fryer cookbook, and I feel that I could write dozens more! Although even in my first book I developed recipes for cookies and cakes and muffins and casseroles, as the air fryer evolves, we can cook things we didn't dream of at first. Using the Instant Vortex Air Fryer you can make moist brownies, crisp granola, deeply browned and tender potatoes, juicy rotisserie chicken, beignets, quiche, paella, chicken satay, beef korma, pizza, scalloped potatoes, crisps and crumbles, cakes, and cookies. The sky's the limit!

With the air fryer, home cooks no longer need to wrestle with hot cooking oil, but that isn't the only advantage of this appliance. "Fried" foods made in the air fryer are healthier than their counterparts cooked in oil because it only takes a little bit of oil, spritzed onto food, to make deeply crisp and crunchy foods that are as satisfying to eat as they are to make. The air fryer uses 90 to 95 percent less oil than deep-frying. Just think of the calories saved! And the air fryer cooks food to perfection in 30 percent less time than a conventional oven. And, in another great improvement over deep-frying, you can season foods in the air fryer. Marinated chicken breasts and pork tenderloin have beautiful brown crusts and turn out tender and juicy when cooked in this appliance.

This book is designed for the Instant Vortex Plus 10-Quart Air Fryer. With this model, you can use the included rotisserie basket to turn out crisp chicken wings, roasted cauliflower florets, and even sausages and roasted potatoes. The rotisserie spit and forks let you make a burnished and tender chicken just like restaurants do! Although this book uses the Instant Vortex Plus 10-Quart Air Fryer, no matter which version of the Instant Vortex you have, you will find plenty to love in these pages. If you don't have the rotisserie function, you can still roast a beautiful chicken or make fabulously crispy French fries.

The air fryer was first introduced in 2010 in Europe. It quickly became popular and was introduced in the United States soon after. The air fryer has evolved from that little barrel-shaped oven with the big basket (which I still have and use, by the way) to a multi-use appliance like the Instant Vortex. These larger oven-type air fryers give home cooks so much more versatility. With the Instant Vortex you can bake, roast, air fry, rotisserie cook, broil, dehydrate, and reheat with just the touch of a button!

This company began by making the Instant Pot, a combination slow cooker and pressure cooker that can also steam food, cook rice, and bake. This product was an instant hit. (Pun intended.) Home cooks discovered that one appliance could accomplish many kitchen tasks. The success of these multifunctional products made expanding their line into air fryers a natural idea. And the Instant Vortex Plus 10-Quart, which is an oven-style air fryer, transformed the traditional small air fryer into a true kitchen appliance that can air fry, bake, cook, dehydrate, rotisserie cook, and warm—all in one place.

The recipes in this book range from quick and easy breakfast ideas to satisfying appetizers, flavorful main dishes, tempting sides, and some of the best desserts around. These recipes are healthier and easier versions of your favorites. Let's get started so you can discover all the wonderful ways the Instant Vortex will make your life easier.

✦

# CHAPTER ONE

# A COMPLETE GUIDE TO THE INSTANT VORTEX

Even if you have other air fryers, it's important that you take some time to learn about this particular Vortex model. In this chapter, I cover how air frying works, discuss how the Instant Vortex is different from other versions, look at the functions of this appliance, show you how to get started with your new air fryer, and take an in-depth look at the functions so you can get the most out of this fabulous machine. I also cover safety tips and troubleshooting options and tell you about helpful kitchen tools and how to care for and clean your new appliance.

# Air Frying and More

When you buy an air fryer, you expect it to, well, fry food! But the Instant Vortex Air Fryer is so much more than a basic air fryer. This machine takes the air fryer's versatility to a completely new level, adding the functions of **bake**, **broil**, **dehydrate**, **reheat**, **roast**, and **rotisserie**. And although most ovens with a rotisserie function only let you spit-roast food, the Instant Vortex has a rotisserie basket that opens up the world of air frying. Just think—using the rotisserie function, you don't have to turn chicken wings, French fries, or cauliflower florets as they cook to get evenly browned, beautifully tender results. The basket does all the work for you! For instance, make Bacon-Mustard Rotisserie Chicken (page 82), Crispy French Fries (page 56), Deconstructed Apple Crisp (page 109), and Shrimp and Peppers (page 69) with the rotisserie forks and basket at the touch of a button. Or try making Rice and Meatball–Stuffed Peppers (page 93), Sweet and Hot Chicken Wings (page 51), or Chocolate Peanut Butter Molten Cupcakes (page 113) using the oven racks. Is your mouth watering yet?

There are several versions of the Instant Vortex Air Fryer. The recipes in this book were designed for the popular Instant Vortex Plus 10-Quart, so if you have another model you will need to make small adjustments. The Pro models add the Toast and Warm functions, which are useful for making breakfast or holding food when family members eat at different times. The traditionally shaped Instant Vortex air fryers do not have a rotisserie function. But this book will give you instructions to make rotisserie recipes in those models. And there are two sizes of the Instant Vortex oven-style air fryers; the only difference is capacity.

# Five Benefits of the Instant Vortex

1. **Air frying is a healthier way to cook than deep-frying.** An average serving of deep-fried French fries contains 300 calories and 15 grams of fat. An average serving of air fried French fries has just 180 calories and 5 grams of fat. Shocking, isn't it? But the health benefits don't end with simple calorie and fat reductions. Heating oils to the high temperatures used in deep-frying can also create trans fats, which increase your risk of developing diseases such as diabetes and heart disease. Air frying eliminates that risk.

2. **Food cooks more quickly in an air fryer.** The air fryer uses a fan to move hot air around the food, so it cooks up to 30 percent faster than in a conventional oven. Over time, that adds up to a lot of minutes you don't have to spend in the kitchen!

3. **Cooking and baking in the air fryer is so easy.** Unlike cooking on the stovetop, or deep-frying for that matter, you don't have to pay attention to the food as it cooks. Just check it when the end of the cooking time approaches. You may have to turn the food over or rearrange it, but most times the air fryer takes care of everything while you relax or make other foods to complete your meal.

4. **You can cook foods in this air fryer that you wouldn't expect.** Have you ever thought about roasting apples on a rotisserie spit to make a Deconstructed Apple Crisp (page 109)? How about making a stir-fry or risotto in an air fryer? The versatility of this appliance means you don't have to limit yourself when cooking in it.

5. **Baked goods turn out beautifully in the air fryer.** Cookies are perfectly and evenly browned and tender. Brownies are moist with a crackly top. Cakes rise to great heights and are tender and moist. The fan circulates air around these foods, so everything turns out amazing. Every single time.

## How Air Frying Works

The air fryer is an ingenious appliance. It's basically a convection oven, but smaller, so the heat is concentrated to create the results we want. A fan blows hot air around the interior. This helps dry the surface of food, so it browns and crisps evenly and quickly in a process called non-enzymatic browning (also known as the Maillard reaction). And the air movement cooks the interior of the food at the same time, so it finishes cooking to a safe temperature by the time the outside is crisp. Whether you use an oven-style air fryer or a basket-style air fryer, the mechanism and results are the same. The racks and baskets in the air fryer are perforated so air can move freely around the food. In the basket-type appliance, you usually need to shake the basket to redistribute the food so it cooks evenly. The oven-style air fryers use perforated racks so no shaking is required, but you may need to rearrange or turn the food while it cooks.

## Getting Started with the Instant Vortex

Let's look at the Instant Vortex Air Fryer more closely so you can feel comfortable using it right out of the box. The sooner you get started, the sooner you can begin making delicious food!

First, unpack your air fryer. Remove all the packing material from the air fryer, both inside and out. Sit down and read the instruction booklet, cover to cover. You'll need to wash the racks and the rotisserie basket, along with the forks and rod for rotisserie cooking. You should also wipe the inside of the air fryer with a damp cloth to make sure everything is sparkling clean. Then find a space for the air fryer. Do not put it on the stovetop. It should be on a solid surface, with at least 5 inches of clearance at the back, sides, and top of the appliance. Look at all the buttons; read what each function does; and familiarize yourself with assembling and inserting the rotisserie equipment and the racks.

Do a practice run, or initial test run, as described in this paragraph (and in the instruction booklet). This is important for two reasons: There is often a light plastic smell when you first use the air fryer; the practice run burns that off. The smell isn't harmful, but you may want to open a window. And second, you'll know just how to use this wonderful appliance when you're ready to cook. To begin the practice run, touch Air Fry, then set the timer for 20 minutes. Let the appliance work. When Add Food lights up, open the door and add the racks and trays. Close the door and choose the cooking time and temperature again. Let the timer run down. When the cooking program ends, touch Cancel.

Lastly, I would recommend reading through a few recipes in this book. "Walk" through the steps, practicing inserting the rotisserie basket and racks in the air fryer and adding pans. Don't turn the oven on during this time—just get used to the feel of the appliance.

## Use and Settings

When you're ready to cook, be sure to read through the recipe first. Make sure you have all the ingredients and utensils on hand, and prepare the food. Each recipe indicates which function to use, along with the time and temperature settings. Some recipes use the Smart Program buttons (Air Fry, Bake, Broil, Dehydrate, Reheat, Roast).

To wake the air fryer, touch any button. To preheat, set the function you will use, and then adjust the cooking temperature, if necessary, and set the timer. Touch Start, the display will read On, and the oven will begin preheating. This time does not count in the cooking time.

When the oven is preheated and ready, the display will say Add Food. Place the food on the rack or racks or add pans. Hit the Light button so you can see the food as it cooks. Close the door and cooking will begin. Halfway through the cooking time, the display will read Turn Food. Open the door (the timer will pause) and turn or rotate or rearrange the food as the recipe instructs. Return the food to the oven and close the door; cooking will resume.

When the timer beeps and the display reads End, check the food for doneness according to the recipe instructions, using a food thermometer, if required. If you need to add cooking time, set the temperature again and add a few minutes to the timer. Then add the food and cook or bake until done.

You can customize each smart program to your specifications if you make one recipe repeatedly. Select a smart program, then use the + / − Time and Temperature keys until they reach the settings you want. Touch Start and those numbers will be saved. The next time you want to make that food, just touch that smart program button and you don't have to do another thing. To reset a smart program, when the air fryer is in standby mode, touch and hold the smart program key for 5 seconds. The time and temperature will be restored to factory default settings.

## Air Fry

The Air Fry function is used to make wonderful recipes like Crispy French Fries (page 56) and Shrimp and Grilled Cheese Sandwiches (page 37). The perforated racks are used for this function. This function is also used to cook frozen foods, such as chicken nuggets and sweet potato fries. Check the air fryer chart at the end of this book for cooking times and temperatures for those foods.

Hot air circulates around the food as it cooks, reaching every nook and cranny to make super-crisp and beautifully browned results. The default temperature for the Air Fry function is 400°F and the default time is 18 minutes, but you can change that if the recipe calls for it or if you want to cook at a different temperature. The time range is 1 minute to 1 hour.

Most air fry recipes ask you to dry any moist foods so they brown better. Use a paper towel to blot the food until it is mostly dry before cooking. And most recipes instruct you to spritz or mist the food with a bit of cooking oil to aid browning and crisping and to boost flavor and help crumbs and seasoning stick to the food. In some recipes, the food may be coated with breadcrumbs, grated cheese, flour, or cornmeal to create a crisp and flavorful crust.

And you will most likely need to turn or rearrange the food halfway through cooking time to ensure even cooking and browning. The air fryer will tell you when to do this.

## Roast

Roasting is cooking food using a high temperature for a longer period. Most foods that are roasted are larger, such as a beef roast or a whole chicken. The convection function of the air fryer makes roasting a breeze and creates meats that are deeply browned, with a crisp crust and juicy interior. Roasted vegetables become sweet and tender with a wonderful crispness. You can use the Roast function for beef, casseroles, lamb, pork, poultry, and vegetables. The high heat browns the food and aids caramelization, which happens when proteins and sugars on the food's surface interact to produce flavor compounds and browning. My favorite roasted recipes in this book include Roasted Bell Peppers with Garlic (page 54) and Roasted Veggie Chicken Salad (page 76).

The default temperature for roasting is 380°F, but you can change that if the recipe directs you to. The default time for roasting is 40 minutes, but that can also be changed. The time range for this function is 1 minute to 1 hour.

You probably won't need to do anything to the food as it roasts. Most roasted foods do not need to be turned, rearranged, or otherwise manipulated. And you can season foods that you roast any way you'd like, with herbs and spices, dry rubs, marinades, and crusts.

## Broil

Broiling is direct top-down heating. You can cook a recipe completely by broiling, or you can broil a recipe to add a crisp top or to melt cheese for the perfect finishing touch. Think of a broiler as an upside-down grill. You can broil burgers, chicken, chops, fish fillets, kabobs, or vegetables for wonderful flavor and crunch. Make nachos or toasted cheese sandwiches with this function.

The Broil function cooks food at 400°F. You cannot vary the temperature for this function; it is set and automatic. The time range for broiling is from 1 to 40 minutes. This time is shorter than other functions in this book because the intense heat of the broiler cooks very quickly and can burn food. Watch the food carefully when broiling so it doesn't overcook or burn, which produces acrid, unpalatable flavors. Broiling is the fastest cooking method.

My favorite recipes in this book that use the Broil function are Tex-Mex Turkey Burgers (page 81) and Broiled Curried Fruit (page 104). In fact, pair them for a fabulous meal!

Foods do not need to be as dry for broiling as they do for air frying, simply because the heat is more direct. Even moist foods like cheese will brown when broiled. The browning and caramelization that happen under the broiler are intense. And use thinner cuts of meat when broiling; steaks and chops should be 1 inch thick or less so they cook to a safe internal temperature by the time the exterior is browned and caramelized.

## Bake

Baking is simply dry heat cooking. The temperatures used in baking are lower than temperatures for broiling or roasting. Although you can bake casseroles, fish, and poultry, this function is most often used for brownies, cakes, cookies, crisps, crumbles, and muffins.

My favorite baked recipes in this book are Marble Cheesecake (page 107) for a fabulous dessert, and Double Berry Muffins (page 25) for a special breakfast or brunch.

The default temperature for baking is 380°F, although many recipes call for a lower temperature, usually 325°F to 350°F. The time range is from 1 minute to 1 hour.

Baked goods are more delicate than other types of food cooked in the air fryer. It's important to get batters and doughs into the air fryer quickly after they are made so the result is light and fluffy. Use double-acting baking powder, which reacts first when liquid is added, then again when the batter is heated, for the highest loft.

When making cookies and cakes, watch baking times carefully. Check the food at the earliest time to make sure these items don't overcook or get too brown, or they will be dry and tough. Remember that convection cooking happens faster than cooking in a conventional oven.

The most common doneness test for baked goods is to use a toothpick or your finger. For the toothpick test, insert it into the cake or brownie near the center. If the toothpick comes out clean, or with just a few moist crumbs attached, your food is done. For some recipes, you will be asked to touch the surface of the cake lightly. If it springs back and leaves no indentation, it's done.

## Reheat

Most people dread the word "leftover." Not with the Instant Vortex Air Fryer! This function reheats food beautifully without overcooking it. Pizzas have a crisp crust when reheated in the air fryer, and the cheese stays melted and creamy. Casseroles are piping hot and never dry; the Reheat function brings out their flavor and makes them taste fresh baked. Reheated chicken is juicy and delicious with a wonderfully crisp crust. And reheated baked goods are tender and fluffy, never dry or tough.

The Reheat default temperature is set at 280°F, but you can increase or decrease it. This temperature is best for reheating foods so they are safe to eat but still delicious with the perfect texture. The time range is from 1 minute to 1 hour. You just need to put the food on a perforated rack in the oven. Thinner foods will obviously take less time to reheat than thicker foods. Use a lower temperature for thicker foods so the exterior doesn't dry out before the interior is hot. Don't overcrowd the pan so the food reheats evenly. Start with 5 minutes of reheating time and add more time in 2- to 3-minute intervals until the internal temperature of the food reaches 165°F, measured with a food thermometer, for food-safety reasons.

You can reheat any recipe in this book using this particular function, but I love reheating Bacon-Garlic Pizza (page 100) and Chicken Tenders with Veggies (page 87).

## Dehydrate

Dehydrating is a wonderful way to preserve food and make healthy snacks. You'll save money, too, since you don't have to buy expensive dehydrated food that is often made with a lot of chemicals and preservatives.

The Dehydrate default setting is 120°F and the time range is from 1 to 72 hours. This temperature is low enough to remove the moisture from food so the water activity is reduced, and it will be difficult for bacteria to grow. Foods you can dehydrate include thin strips of fruit, meat, and vegetables and leathers and more. My favorite dehydrating foods in this book are Spicy Beef Jerky Dip (page 48) and Strawberry-Lime Fruit Leather (page 111).

The most important tip for dehydrating is to put the food in a single layer. If you stack or layer food, it will not dry evenly and bacteria or mold may grow. Use the perforated racks to make sure that air circulates evenly around the food.

Rinse, dry, and slice fruits and vegetables to dehydrate them. To make leathers, the fruits or vegetables are blended, then the mixture is spread onto parchment paper in special dehydrator trays. The leather is done when it's no longer sticky. All dehydrated products should be stored in airtight containers at room temperature, but they can be frozen for longer storage.

## Rotate

The rotisserie function uses Rotate. This function is only available on the Instant Vortex Plus (for those that don't have that model, you'll find tips on making those recipes using your oven racks). This is the most exciting function of this appliance, in my opinion!

You can rotisserie cook foods at any temperature, but the default setting is 350°F. And you can rotisserie cook for 1 minute to 1 hour. My favorite rotisserie recipes in this book include Deconstructed Apple Crisp (page 109) and Bacon-Mustard Rotisserie Chicken (page 82). Those two recipes would make an incredible dinner and dessert combo.

The recipes indicate whether you need to use the basket or the spit to cook the food. To use the basket, put the food in the basket before you preheat the air fryer. Preheat the air fryer, then add the basket. You should use hot pads or oven gloves to protect your hands.

Align the tab on the basket with the notch on the lid, then put the lid on the basket. Turn the lid clockwise to secure it. To use the spit, unscrew the setting screws and remove the forks from the rod. Push the spit through the food. Slide the forks back onto the food, making sure the prongs are securely inserted into the food on both sides. Turn the setting screws to hold the food in place.

Open the door and slide the basket or spit into the guides, using the air fryer rotisserie tool. Move the red rotisserie catch lever to the right and hold it in position. Align the left side of the basket or spit with the hole in the catch and set the right side in the other catch. Release the catch lever. Rotate the basket or spit to make sure it's secure. The catch should move with the basket or spit. If it doesn't, keep rotating it until it is secure. Close the oven door, select Start to begin, then touch Rotate. Let the food cook until it is done according to the recipe instructions.

To remove the basket or spit, open the oven door. Put oven gloves on your hands again. Put the hooks on the rotisserie lift under the left and right arms of the basket or spit. Move the catch lever to the right and hold it to release the basket or spit. Pull the accessory toward you, then release the lever. Remove the basket or spit with the food and put it on a level heat-resistant surface. Remove the food from the basket or pull the food from the spit and serve.

Some recipes call for placing a pan underneath the spit or basket to cook more than one food at the same time. You may use the drip pan, or a shallow rimmed sheet pan. Add and remove the pan using tongs or oven gloves.

# Safety Tips

Follow these tips so you can safely enjoy using your Instant Vortex Air Fryer and the recipes you make.

1. **Always use tongs to remove food.** As with any cooking appliance, the food will be very hot when it is ready to eat. Use tongs to remove the food so you don't burn your hands.

2. **Always use hot pads or oven gloves to remove the rotisserie spit and basket from the air fryer.** The metal basket, spit, and forks will be blazing hot after use. Always use hot pads or gloves. And let these items cool completely before you wash them.

3. **Put a heat-resistant pad on the open oven door.** When you are adding pans to the air fryer, think about putting a heat-resistant pad on the oven door to protect your hands against burns. You may want to use tongs to add and remove the pad to further protect yourself.

4. **Keep space between the air fryer, walls, and overhead cabinets.** The air fryer needs at least five inches of space between the appliance and walls and overhead cabinets. Also think about using a vent fan while the appliance is working.

5. **Never leave the air fryer unattended.** Food can burn if cooked too long. And the outside surfaces can get very hot. You don't want your kids or unsuspecting adults to touch the appliance while it's working.

6. **Always cook foods to safe final internal temperatures.** The USDA has charts of the temperatures that egg, fish, ground meat, meat, and poultry dishes should reach so they are safe to eat; a general guide is to cook ground meats to 160°F, ground poultry, including ground turkey and chicken, to 165°F, beef and pork roasts to 145°F, fish to 145°F, egg dishes to 160°F, and chicken and turkey cuts to 165°F.

## Cleaning and Care

First, the air fryer must be completely cool before cleaning. Unplug it from the wall socket. Never use harsh chemicals, powders, or scouring pads to clean the interior or exterior of this appliance. The drip pan, cooking trays, rotisserie spit and basket, and rotisserie lift tool are all dishwasher safe, or you can clean them by immersing them in soapy water. Clean the cooking chamber, the removable door, and the unit's exterior with a clean damp cloth. You can clean the heating coil with a damp cloth, but make sure it is dry before using the air fryer again.

If you need to remove the door for cleaning, put one hand on top of the appliance. Open the oven door at a 45-degree angle and pull it up from the right side until it pops off. To reinstall it, hold the oven door at a 45-degree angle to the appliance and align the teeth at the bottom of the door with the grooves in the air fryer. Press down on the right side of the door until it pops into place, then press the left side down.

When you are using the air fry, roast, reheat, and rotisserie functions, make sure you always use the drip pan on the floor of the air fryer to catch any drippings or you'll have a mess on your hands.

# Tips and Troubleshooting

If you are having trouble getting the results you want, these tips and troubleshooting ideas will help.

**Don't overcrowd the pans or the basket with food.** Hot air needs to circulate around the food for proper browning and crisping. If your food isn't evenly brown or crisp, overcrowding is probably the issue. The rotisserie basket, for instance, should only be filled 75 percent full at most. This is why many recipes call for putting food on one or more racks in a single layer.

**If smoke is coming from the air fryer, the issue depends on the color of the smoke.** White smoke means you are probably cooking food with a high fat content, such as burgers or sausages. The white "smoke" could also be steam, or seasoning or crumbs on the food may have blown into the heating element. When you are done cooking, clean the heating element.

If the smoke is black, there is a problem. You may be using oil with a low smoke point, such as olive oil, and the oil is burning. There could be food residue on the heating coil or in the cooking chamber. Or there could be an issue with the air fryer, such as a faulty circuit or heating element. Unplug the appliance and take it to a repair shop or contact customer care.

**The unit is plugged in but will not turn on.** It's possible that a fuse or circuit breaker has tripped. Or the plug may not be pushed all the way into the outlet, or the oven door may be open.

**The lights all flash and a code appears on the display.** This is a problem that means there could be a temperature sensor issue or a short circuit in the sensor. Contact customer care.

**The food isn't crisp and brown.** There could be several reasons for this problem. First, the basket or pans could be overcrowded so the heat isn't reaching all the pieces evenly. Or the food may be too wet; to fix this, pat food dry with paper towels or sprinkle with a bit of flour or cornstarch.

**Coating and seasonings come off the food while it's cooking.** You may want to spray the food with some oil or other liquid before you add seasonings and coatings, so they stick. Press coatings, such as breadcrumbs, onto the food so they stay on as air circulates.

**The food burns or has an unpleasant odor.** If this happens, reduce the cooking time and temperature the next time you make a recipe. Or an unpleasant odor could be the result of food residue left in the appliance or on the heating coil. Clean the air fryer thoroughly before the next use.

**Food sticks to the air fryer.** Spritz the food with a little bit of oil. Or, next time, spray the basket or the pan with a bit of cooking oil before adding the food. You can also use perforated parchment paper to line the racks.

# Helpful Kitchen Tools

Although you don't need any special tools to make lots of recipes in your air fryer, some of these utensils make cooking easier and more fun.

**Baking pans and sheets:** Because the air fryer is smaller than an oven, you will need smaller pans and sheets. The 10-quart version can hold a 7-inch round or square pan, whereas smaller air fryers may only accommodate a 6-inch size. A springform pan is a good purchase, since you can use the bottom as a baking sheet. A 7 × 9-inch rimmed sheet pan is also a good purchase.

**Heat-resistant pad:** You may want this pad to place on the open oven door to shield your wrist and arm as you add and remove pans from the air fryer. It's especially helpful when you add the drip pan or a baking sheet to the bottom of the air fryer.

**Hot pads and oven gloves:** These are essential kitchen accessories. Use them to add pans to the hot oven and to remove rotisserie accessories, sheets, and pans.

**Oil mister:** Some recipes call for spraying or misting the food with oil before it's cooked to aid in browning. An oil mister lets you control the amount you add.

**Silicone muffin tins and baking pans:** These items are great for making muffins and cupcakes and turn out perfect cakes and coffeecakes. A 4- or 6-cup muffin tin will fit into the Vortex 10 Air Fryer. An 8-inch metal bowl will fit into the air fryer; it should be about 3 inches deep.

**Silicone spatulas:** You'll use these to turn food and to remove food from pans and baking sheets. They should be made from heatproof silicone so they don't scratch the air fryer oven racks or nonstick pans.

**Tongs:** Using tongs is essential to remove hot food from the appliance, and to rearrange food during cooking. Tongs are also good for turning some foods. Buy spring-loaded tongs, which are easier to use.

# About the Recipes

The recipes in this book were developed for the Instant Vortex 10-Quart Air Fryer and most recipes will serve 4 to 6. You can make these recipes in other sizes of air fryers from this brand, but you will probably need to reduce quantities and cooking times. To do this, adjust by volume.

For instance, if a recipe calls for an 8 × 2-inch pan, which holds 6 cups, and your air fryer will only fit a 6 × 2-inch pan, which holds 4 cups, multiply each ingredient by $\frac{2}{3}$ (0.6666). Round up or down if the amount is a fraction, such as 1.8 or 1.2 tablespoons. For timing, reduce the cooking time for smaller pan sizes by 20 percent and check the food for doneness at the earliest time in the cooking range. When making casseroles or cooking meats, simply double or halve the recipe in most cases. For instance, if a casserole recipe made in a small air fryer serves 2, double it for use in the Instant Vortex 10-Quart to serve 4. If a recipe serves 4, halve it to serve 2. You can easily cook 4 to 6 chicken breasts, burgers, or pork chops in the Instant Vortex 10-Quart Air Fryer.

Many recipes include a label indicating that it is appropriate for people on special diets. The labels are Dairy-Free, Gluten-Free, Vegan, and Vegetarian. Dairy-free recipes do not use butter, buttermilk, cheese, cream, milk, sour cream, or yogurt. Gluten-free recipes contain no wheat for people with celiac disease or people who are allergic to that ingredient. Vegan recipes use no animal products, including butter, eggs, and honey. Vegetarian recipes do not use any fish, meat, poultry, or Parmesan cheese. Many recipes will have a tip with variations you can make or more information about the ingredients used in the recipe.

When you make a recipe from this book, make it first as directed. You can then branch out and experiment, using different foods or substituting your favorite ingredients for the ones called for. Above all, enjoy cooking these recipes and have fun.

*Scotch Eggs, page 21*

✦

# CHAPTER TWO

# BREAKFASTS AND BRUNCHES

# Asparagus Bell Pepper Strata

**Serves 4 to 6**

Setting: **Bake** • Temperature: **330°F** • Prep time: **12 minutes** • Cook time: **23 minutes**

*A strata is a casserole made with bread, veggies, and cheese baked in a rich egg custard. You can use just about any leftover vegetable you have on hand for this recipe; then you can skip the first step where you cook the asparagus and red bell pepper. Serve this strata with orange juice and coffee.*

6 asparagus spears, cut
  into 2-inch pieces
½ cup chopped red bell
  pepper
1 tablespoon water
Nonstick cooking spray
3 slices whole wheat
  bread, cut into ½-inch
  cubes
6 large eggs
¼ cup whole milk
Pinch salt
Freshly ground black
  pepper
1 cup grated Havarti or
  Swiss cheese
2 tablespoons chopped
  fresh flat-leaf parsley
2 tablespoons grated
  Parmesan cheese

1. Preheat the air fryer by setting it to Bake and the temperature to 330°F.

2. In a 7-inch baking pan, combine the asparagus, bell pepper, and water and place the pan on the lower rack. Bake for 3 to 5 minutes, or until crisp-tender. Move the vegetables to a plate and drain the water from the pan.

3. Spray the pan with cooking spray. Arrange the bread cubes and cooked vegetables in the pan and set aside.

4. In a medium bowl, whisk the eggs with the milk, salt, and pepper until combined. Add the Havarti cheese and parsley. Pour the eggs into the baking pan over the bread mixture. Sprinkle with the Parmesan cheese.

5. Bake for 12 to 18 minutes, or until the eggs are set and the top starts to brown.

VARIATION TIP: Other vegetables you can use include cooked green beans, chopped potatoes, corn, or baby peas. Or try a combination of your favorites. You can also use different types of cheese, from Cheddar to Provolone.

# Scotch Eggs

Serves **4 to 6** • DAIRY-FREE

Setting: **Air Fry** • Temperature: **370°F** • Prep time: **15 minutes** • Cook time: **13 minutes**

*Scotch eggs is a classic English recipe made with a hard-boiled egg encased in pork sausage and deep-fried. This recipe is lightened up using chicken sausage and "frying" it in the air fryer. If desired, garnish with cilantro for an extra kick of flavor. Serve with a fruit salad and muffins.*

1½ pounds bulk lean chicken or turkey sausage

3 large eggs, divided

1½ cups dried breadcrumbs, divided

½ cup all-purpose flour

6 large hard-boiled eggs, peeled

Olive oil, for misting

INGREDIENT TIP: Buy hard-boiled eggs, already peeled, at many grocery stores or hard-boil them in your air fryer at 270°F for 17 minutes.

1. In a large bowl, combine the sausage, 1 egg, and ½ cup of breadcrumbs and mix well. Divide the mixture into 6 pieces and flatten each into a long oval on wax paper.

2. In a shallow bowl, beat the remaining 2 eggs. Put the flour on a plate. Put the remaining 1 cup of breadcrumbs on another plate.

3. Roll each hard-boiled egg in the flour, then wrap a sausage oval around each to encase the eggs.

4. Roll the sausage-encased eggs in the flour, then in the beaten egg, and then in the breadcrumbs. Press the breadcrumbs into the sausage firmly.

5. Preheat the air fryer by setting it to Air Fry and the temperature to 370°F.

6. Place the eggs in a single layer on a rack in the air fryer and mist with oil.

7. Air fry for 6 minutes, then carefully turn the eggs with tongs and mist with oil again. Air fry for 5 to 7 minutes more, or until the sausage is thoroughly cooked to 165°F and browned.

# Omelet in a Bread Cup

Serves **4 to 6**

Setting: **Bake** • Temperature: **330°F** • Prep time: **12 minutes** • Cook time: **13 minutes**

*An omelet served inside a bread cup is a fun twist on a breakfast classic. The rolls become so crisp and toasted on the outside, while the eggs are moist and fluffy. You can use your favorite type of cheese in this recipe, or add other ingredients, such as cooked vegetables.*

6 (3 × 4-inch) crusty rolls

6 thin slices Swiss or Cheddar cheese

7 large eggs

¼ cup heavy (whipping) cream

1 teaspoon dried thyme leaves

Pinch salt

Freshly ground black pepper

2 tablespoons grated Parmesan cheese

1. Preheat the air fryer by setting it to Bake and the temperature to 330°F.

2. Cut off the tops of the rolls and remove some of the insides with your fingers to make a shell, leaving about ½ inch of the bread on the sides. Reserve the breadcrumbs for another use.

3. Line each roll with 1 slice of cheese, pressing it down gently so the cheese covers the inside of the rolls.

4. In a medium bowl, whisk the eggs, heavy cream, thyme, salt, and pepper to taste until combined. Spoon the eggs into the rolls over the cheese. Sprinkle with the Parmesan cheese. Place the rolls on a rack or two in the air fryer in a single layer.

5. Bake for 8 to 13 minutes, or until the egg mixture is puffy and starts to brown on top. The temperature of the eggs should be at least 160°F on a food thermometer.

   VARIATION TIP: For a non-vegetarian version, add 3 cooked, crispy, crumbled bacon slices or ⅓ cup diced ham to the egg mixture.

# Salmon and Rice Frittata

Serves **4 to 6**  •  GLUTEN-FREE

Setting: **Bake**  •  Temperature: **320°F**  •  Prep time: **15 minutes**  •  Cook time: **20 minutes**

*A frittata is a sturdier version of an omelet that can be eaten hot or cold.
This wonderful gluten-free breakfast is rich and hearty. You can make it even
easier by using leftover rice or rice from your favorite restaurant. Or use
frozen rice; just thaw it by running hot water over the package.*

6 large eggs

2 tablespoons heavy
(whipping) cream

1 teaspoon dried basil
leaves

⅛ teaspoon kosher salt

Nonstick cooking spray

1 cup cooked rice

1 (5-ounce) can salmon,
drained and flaked

1 cup baby spinach leaves

⅔ cup grated Monterey
Jack or Cojack cheese

2 tablespoons grated
Parmesan cheese

1. Preheat the air fryer by setting it to Bake and the
   temperature to 320°F.

2. In a medium bowl, whisk the eggs, heavy cream,
   basil, and salt until frothy. Coat a 7-inch square
   baking pan with cooking spray.

3. In the prepared pan, combine the rice, salmon,
   spinach, and Monterey Jack cheese. Pour in the
   egg mixture and sprinkle with the Parmesan.

4. Place the pan on the lower rack and bake for 16 to
   20 minutes, or until the frittata is puffed and
   golden brown.

INGREDIENT TIP: If you can't find canned salmon in
a 5-ounce can, buy the larger 14½-ounce size and use
one-third of it for this recipe. The remaining salmon
can be refrigerated or frozen for later use. Add it to a
pasta salad or toss with a green salad for an easy lunch.

# Cheesy Sausage Egg Bites

Serves **4** • GLUTEN-FREE

Setting: **Bake** • Temperature: **350°F** • Prep time: **10 minutes** • Cook time: **22 minutes**

*Egg bites are a popular breakfast item available at many restaurants and easy to make in your air fryer! The sausages brown and heat to crisp and juicy perfection, then are chopped and baked into puffy little egg "muffins." This is a great way to get breakfast on the table in a hurry with minimal effort.*

3 frozen precooked
  breakfast sausages
5 large eggs
3 tablespoons sour cream
½ teaspoon dried basil
  leaves
¼ teaspoon kosher salt
Freshly ground black
  pepper
Nonstick baking spray
½ cup minced red bell
  pepper
½ cup grated Colby
  cheese
1 tablespoon chopped
  fresh flat-leaf parsley

1. Preheat the air fryer by setting it to Bake and the temperature to 350°F.

2. Put the sausages on the lower rack and air fry for 8 to 10 minutes, or until they reach an internal temperature of 165°F. Remove from the air fryer and let cool while you prepare the eggs.

3. In a large glass measuring cup for easy pouring, whisk the eggs, sour cream, basil, salt, and pepper to taste.

4. Coat a 4-cup muffin tin with baking spray. Cut the sausages into ¼-inch pieces and divide them among the prepared muffin cups along with the bell pepper.

5. Pour the egg mixture over the sausage mixture and sprinkle with the Colby cheese.

6. Bake for 8 to 12 minutes, or until the egg cups are puffy and 160°F. Sprinkle with the parsley and serve.

VARIATION TIP: If you have a basket-type air fryer, use individual silicone muffin cups. Coat the cups with nonstick baking spray before you add the food and put them into the air fryer basket before you add the sausages, bell pepper, and eggs.

# Double Berry Muffins

Serves **4 to 6** • VEGETARIAN

Setting: **Bake** • Temperature: **320°F** • Prep time: **15 minutes** • Cook time: **17 minutes**

*Muffins are the perfect choice for breakfast. And this sweet and easy recipe uses blueberries and raspberries for color and flavor. You can double this recipe and store the extras covered at room temperature for a great midday snack.*

1 cup all-purpose flour, plus 1 tablespoon

3 tablespoons granulated sugar

1 tablespoon brown sugar

1½ teaspoons baking powder

½ cup whole milk

¼ cup safflower oil

1 large egg

2 tablespoons sour cream

⅓ cup fresh or frozen raspberries

⅓ cup fresh or frozen blueberries

Nonstick baking spray

1. Preheat the air fryer by setting it to Bake and the temperature to 320°F.

2. In a medium bowl, combine 1 cup of flour, the granulated sugar, brown sugar, and baking powder and mix until combined.

3. In a small bowl, combine the milk, oil, egg, and sour cream and mix well. Stir the egg mixture into the flour mixture just until combined.

4. In another small bowl, toss the raspberries and blueberries with the remaining 1 tablespoon of flour until coated. Stir the berries gently into the batter.

5. Coat a 6-cup muffin tin with baking spray or line it with paper liners. Spoon the batter into the prepared cups, filling each three-quarters full.

6. Bake for 12 to 17 minutes, or until the tops of the muffins spring back when lightly touched with your finger. Cool on a wire rack for 10 minutes before serving.

INGREDIENT TIP: You can use frozen raspberries and blueberries in this recipe, but don't thaw them before serving or the berries will leak into the batter and make the muffins too wet and will also stain the batter.

# Cranberry and Almond Beignets

Makes **16 beignets** • VEGETARIAN

Setting: **Air Fry** • Temperature: **330°F** • Prep time: **15 minutes**

Cook time: **8 minutes per batch**

*Beignets were made famous in the United States at the Café du Monde in New Orleans. That restaurant serves the little puffs with chicory coffee. These beignets, which are crisp and slightly sweet, are studded with sweet and tart dried cranberries and crunchy almonds.*

1½ cups all-purpose flour

3 tablespoons brown sugar

2 teaspoons baking soda

⅛ teaspoon salt

¼ cup chopped dried cranberries

2 tablespoons chopped slivered almonds

½ cup buttermilk

1 large egg

2 tablespoons unsalted butter, melted

½ cup powdered sugar

INGREDIENT TIP: Make sure to use unsalted butter to coat the dough, because unsalted butter ensures that the dough will not stick to the air fryer rack. Always use unsalted butter to grease pans and baking sheets if you don't use nonstick baking spray.

1. Preheat the air fryer by setting it to Air Fry and the temperature to 330°F.

2. In a medium bowl, combine the flour, brown sugar, baking soda, and salt and mix well. Stir in the cranberries and almonds.

3. In a small bowl, combine the buttermilk and egg and whisk until smooth. Stir the wet ingredients into the dry ingredients until just moistened.

4. Lightly flour a clean work surface and place the dough on it. Pat the dough into an 8 × 8-inch square and cut it into 16 pieces. Coat each piece lightly with butter.

5. Arrange the pieces on the air fryer rack, making sure they don't touch. You may need to use two racks or cook in batches depending on your air fryer.

6. Air fry for 5 to 8 minutes, or until the beignets are puffed and golden brown.

7. Remove the beignets and immediately dunk each into powdered sugar to coat. Serve warm.

# Dutch Pancake

Serves **4**  •  VEGETARIAN

Setting: **Bake**  •  Temperature: **330°F**  •  Prep time: **12 minutes**  •  Cook time: **17 minutes**

*A Dutch pancake is made from a batter that is cooked quickly so it puffs up in the oven. When removed from the oven, it falls, making a natural well that you can fill with just about anything—from scrambled eggs to fruit to lots of butter and syrup.*

2 tablespoons unsalted butter

4 large eggs

⅔ cup all-purpose flour

⅔ cup whole milk

1 teaspoon vanilla extract

1 cup sliced fresh strawberries

1 cup fresh raspberries

2 tablespoons powdered sugar

1. Preheat the air fryer by setting it to Bake and the temperature to 330°F.

2. Place a 7-inch round baking pan on the lowest level of the air fryer. Add the butter and heat for about 2 minutes until it melts.

3. Meanwhile, in a medium bowl, combine the eggs, flour, milk, and vanilla and beat well with an eggbeater or a whisk until combined.

4. Carefully remove the pan from the air fryer and tilt it so the butter covers the bottom evenly. Immediately pour in the batter and put the pan back into the air fryer.

5. Bake for 10 to 15 minutes, or until the pancake is puffed and golden brown.

6. Remove from the oven; the pancake will fall. Top with the berries and powdered sugar and serve immediately.

VARIATION TIP: You can also fill this pancake with a combination of crisply cooked, crumbled bacon or chopped breakfast sausage and scrambled eggs.

# Chocolate Peanut Butter–Filled Doughnut Holes

Makes **24 doughnut holes** • VEGETARIAN

Setting: **Air Fry** • Temperature: **340°F** • Prep time: **12 minutes**

Cook time: **12 minutes per batch**

*What could be better than chocolate and peanut butter, encased in a crispy sweet shell, for breakfast? These little doughnut holes are the perfect recipe for the air fryer. They are coated with powdered sugar for a delicious, sweet treat.*

1 (8-ounce) can
  refrigerated biscuits
2 tablespoons creamy
  peanut butter
48 semisweet chocolate
  chips (scant
  3 tablespoons)
3 tablespoons unsalted
  butter, melted
⅓ cup powdered sugar

1. Preheat the air fryer by setting it to Air Fry and the temperature to 340°F.

2. Separate and cut each biscuit into thirds. Flatten each biscuit piece to about ¼ inch.

3. Spread each piece gently with ¼ teaspoon of peanut butter, leaving a ½-inch border, and top each with 2 chocolate chips. Wrap the dough around the chocolate chips and seal the edges well.

4. Brush each doughnut hole with a bit of butter and place on the lower wire rack, leaving 1 inch of space around each doughnut hole. You may need to cook in batches, depending on the size of your air fryer.

5. Air fry for 8 to 12 minutes, or until the doughnut holes are puffed and golden brown.

6. Remove and coat with powdered sugar; serve warm.

VARIATION TIP: Try different filling flavors of chocolate chips, or even use diced candy bars. Just make sure you don't overfill them, or they will break open while they bake.

*Spinach Quiche, page 35*

◆

# LUNCHES

# Veggies on Toast

Serves **4 to 6** • VEGETARIAN

Setting: **Air Fry, Rotate** • Temperature: **350°F** • Prep time: **12 minutes**

Cook time: **14 minutes**

*Cooking vegetables in the rotisserie basket means you don't have to turn them during the cooking process. And they will be perfectly tender and slightly browned and crisp, the perfect topping for the goat cheese–coated toast. Yum.*

1 red bell pepper, cut into ½-inch strips

1 yellow bell pepper, cut into ½-inch strips

1 small yellow summer squash, sliced into ½-inch rounds

3 scallions, white and green parts, cut into ½-inch pieces

1 tablespoon olive oil

3 tablespoons butter, at room temperature

6 slices French or Italian bread

⅔ cup soft goat cheese

1. Preheat the air fryer by setting it to Air Fry and the temperature to 350°F.

2. In a medium bowl, toss the red and yellow bell peppers, squash, and scallions with the oil and place in the rotisserie basket.

3. Insert the rotisserie basket into the air fryer, set the time for 10 minutes, then press Start and Rotate. If your air fryer does not have a rotisserie function, arrange the vegetables on a rack or in the air fryer basket.

4. When the vegetables are tender and just starting to brown, remove them from the basket.

5. Insert the rack into the lowest level in the air fryer.

6. Spread the butter on the bread slices and place them in the air fryer, buttered-side up. Air fry for 2 to 4 minutes, or until the bread is golden brown.

7. Spread the bread with the goat cheese and top with the vegetables to serve.

VARIATION TIP: Use other types of cheese in this delicious recipe. Try cream cheese, ricotta, Brie slices, or a grated soft cheese like Provolone or mozzarella.

# Jumbo Stuffed Mushrooms

Serves **4 to 6**

Setting: **Bake** • Temperature: **390°F** • Prep time: **12 minutes** • Cook time: **10 minutes**

*Portobello mushrooms are large enough to stuff with quite a bit of filling; the jumbo variety will hold enough to make a great lunch. You can find them in most grocery stores in the produce aisle. The cheesy spinach filling is fragrant with fresh rosemary.*

6 jumbo portobello mushrooms

1 tablespoon olive oil

1 (8-ounce) package cream cheese, at room temperature

½ cup grated Parmesan cheese, divided

1 cup frozen chopped spinach, thawed and drained

½ cup soft, fresh breadcrumbs

½ cup grated Monterey Jack cheese

½ teaspoon minced fresh rosemary leaves

1. Preheat the air fryer by setting it to Bake and the temperature to 390°F.

2. Wipe the mushrooms with a damp cloth. Remove the stems and discard. Using a spoon, carefully scrape out most of the gills.

3. Rub the mushrooms with the oil. Place them on a rimmed sheet pan, hollow-side up, and bake for 3 minutes. Carefully remove the caps because they will contain hot liquid. Drain off the liquid.

4. Meanwhile, in a medium bowl, combine the cream cheese, ¼ cup of Parmesan cheese, the spinach, breadcrumbs, Monterey Jack cheese, and rosemary and mix well. Stuff this mixture into the mushroom caps and sprinkle with the remaining ¼ cup of Parmesan.

5. Put the mushroom caps back onto the pan. Bake for 4 to 7 minutes, or until the filling is hot and the mushroom caps are tender.

INGREDIENT TIP: The gills in these large mushroom caps are tender, but they can become bitter when cooked. They will come out easily using a spoon. Just be careful not to tear or break the mushroom caps while you work.

# Mushroom Pita Pizzas

Serves **4** • VEGETARIAN

Setting: **Bake** • Temperature: **360°F** • Prep time: **12 minutes** • Cook time: **6 minutes**

*Pita bread makes a great crust for a super-quick pizza. The bread becomes crisp and crunchy, and the cheese gets all bubbly and brown in the air fryer. You can use this method to make pizzas with any cooked topping; add more vegetables if you'd like. For a non-vegetarian version, add cooked meat such as pepperoni, cooked ground beef, or even cooked diced chicken or ham.*

½ cup pizza sauce

4 (4-inch) pita breads

1 (4-ounce) jar sliced mushrooms, drained

½ teaspoon dried basil leaves

2 scallions, white and green parts, minced

1⅓ cups shredded Provolone cheese

1 cup sliced grape tomatoes

1. Preheat the air fryer by setting it to Bake and the temperature to 360°F.

2. Divide the pizza sauce among the pita breads and spread the sauce evenly over each pita. Top with the mushrooms, basil, scallions, and Provolone cheese.

3. Place the pitas on the lower rack of the air fryer. Bake for 4 to 6 minutes, or until the cheese is melted and starts to brown. Top with the grape tomatoes and serve.

VARIATION TIP: Canned or jarred pizza sauce is usually found in the pasta aisle of the supermarket. You can substitute ½ cup pasta sauce or tomato sauce mixed with some dried Italian seasoning and some cayenne pepper for a bit of heat.

# Spinach Quiche

Serves **4 to 6** • GLUTEN-FREE

Setting: **Bake** • Temperature: **320°F** • Prep time: **10 minutes** • Cook time: **22 minutes**

*A crustless quiche is not only quick to pull together, but also gluten-free! This delicious version makes a low-fuss lunch and tastes even better the next day, either reheated in the air fryer or eaten cold from the fridge.*

6 large eggs

1 (10-ounce) package frozen spinach, thawed and well drained

1 cup shredded Swiss or Havarti cheese

½ cup heavy (whipping) cream

3 tablespoons honey mustard

1 teaspoon dried thyme leaves

⅛ teaspoon kosher salt

Freshly ground black pepper

Nonstick cooking spray

2 tablespoons grated Parmesan cheese

1. Preheat the air fryer by setting it to Bake and the temperature to 320°F.

2. In a medium bowl, whisk the eggs until frothy. Stir in the spinach, Swiss cheese, heavy cream, honey mustard, thyme, salt, and pepper to taste.

3. Coat a 7-inch round baking pan with cooking spray. Pour the egg mixture into the prepared pan. Sprinkle with the Parmesan cheese.

4. Bake for 18 to 22 minutes, or until the quiche is puffed, light golden brown, and set. Let cool for 5 minutes, then cut into wedges to serve.

INGREDIENT TIP: Drain frozen thawed spinach well or it will add too much liquid to the recipe. Squeeze it with your hands, then wrap the spinach in paper towels and squeeze again.

# English Muffin Tuna and Veggie Sandwiches

Serves **4**

Setting: **Air Fry** • Temperature: **390°F** • Prep time: **8 minutes** • Cook time: **6 minutes**

*There probably isn't an easier recipe on the planet—unless you count cereal! In under 15 minutes and with just a few ingredients, you can enjoy a substantial open-face sandwich made from toasted English muffins, melted cheese, and a zesty tuna salad. Double or triple the tuna salad recipe and keep it on hand for up to four days in the refrigerator to make this dish anytime.*

1 (6-ounce) can chunk light tuna, drained

½ cup chopped celery

2 scallions, white and green parts, sliced

⅓ cup mayonnaise

3 tablespoons mustard

1 tablespoon lemon juice

4 tablespoons (½ stick) butter, at room temperature

3 English muffins, halved with a fork

6 thin slices Provolone or Muenster cheese

1. Preheat the air fryer by setting it to Air Fry and the temperature to 390°F.

2. In a small bowl, stir together the tuna, celery, scallions, mayonnaise, mustard, and lemon juice, mixing well. Set aside.

3. Spread the cut side of each English muffin half with butter. Place the halves, buttered-side up, on the lowest rack in the air fryer. Air fry for 2 to 3 minutes, or until toasted.

4. Top each muffin half with 1 slice of cheese and air fry for 2 to 3 minutes, or until the cheese melts.

5. Remove the muffins from the air fryer and top with the tuna mixture.

VARIATION TIP: Use 1 (6-ounce) can of salmon or crabmeat, drained, in place of the tuna. Or, for a vegetarian version, add 1 cup cubed Colby, Cheddar, or Havarti cheese instead.

# Shrimp and Grilled Cheese Sandwiches

**Makes 4 sandwiches**

Setting: **Air Fry** • Temperature: **400°F** • Prep time: **10 minutes** • Cook time: **7 minutes**

*In the air fryer, you can make a grilled cheese sandwich without having to flip it halfway through the cooking time. And you don't have to babysit the sandwiches, checking the bottoms for doneness. And you can cook more than one at a time! What are you waiting for?*

2 cups shredded Colby, Cheddar, or Havarti cheese

2 (4-ounce) cans tiny shrimp, drained

3 tablespoons minced scallion, white and green parts

⅓ cup mayonnaise

8 slices whole-grain or whole wheat bread

4 tablespoons (½ stick) butter, at room temperature

1. Preheat the air fryer by setting it to Air Fry and the temperature to 400°F.

2. In a medium bowl, stir together the cheese, shrimp, scallion, and mayonnaise, mixing well. Spread this mixture on 4 bread slices. Top with the other 4 slices to make sandwiches.

3. Spread the outsides of the sandwiches with butter.

4. Place the sandwiches on the lowest rack of the air fryer. If you have a smaller air fryer you may have to cook the sandwiches in batches.

5. Air fry for 5 to 7 minutes, or until the bread is browned and crisp and the cheese has melted. Halve and serve warm.

VARIATION TIP: For a vegetarian version, omit the shrimp and increase the shredded cheese to 3 cups. The cooking time remains the same.

# Salmon Croquettes

Serves **4 to 6** • DAIRY-FREE

Setting: **Air Fry** • Temperature: **390°F** • Prep time: **15 minutes** • Cook time: **8 minutes**

*Croquettes are little puffs made with finely chopped meat mixed with bread-crumbs and eggs. The balls or patties are deep-fried, but with the air fryer you can make a guilt-free version of this treat.*

1 (15-ounce) can salmon, drained

1⅔ cups soft, fresh breadcrumbs, divided

1 large egg, beaten

2 tablespoons lemon juice

½ cup minced red bell pepper

1 teaspoon dried basil leaves

Pinch salt

Freshly ground black pepper

2 tablespoons olive oil

1 cup cocktail sauce

1. Preheat the air fryer by setting it to Air Fry and the temperature to 390°F.

2. Remove the skin and bones from the salmon (see tip) and finely flake it.

3. In a medium bowl, combine ⅔ cup of bread-crumbs with the egg and lemon juice; mix well and let stand for 5 minutes.

4. Stir in the salmon, bell pepper, basil, salt, and pepper to taste.

5. On a shallow plate, stir together the remaining 1 cup of breadcrumbs and the oil, mixing well.

6. Form the salmon mixture into 1½-inch round balls and press them firmly with your hands. Roll the balls in the crumb mixture to coat.

7. Place the croquettes on the two racks of the air fryer, leaving about 1 inch of space between each. Air fry for 6 to 8 minutes, or until they are crisp and brown. Serve with cocktail sauce for dipping.

INGREDIENT TIP: The skin and bones in canned salmon are edible, but some people find them unpleas-ant to eat, and they interfere with the texture of the croquettes. Simply pick them out and discard.

# Chicken à la King

Serves **4 to 6**

Setting: **Roast** • Temperature: **350°F** • Prep time: **10 minutes** • Cook time: **23 minutes**

*Chicken à la King is a diner classic, but that doesn't mean you can't enjoy it at home. Tender chicken and fresh veggies are cooked in a white sauce, then served over crusty slices of toasted French bread.*

4 boneless, skinless chicken breasts, cut into 1-inch cubes

12 button mushrooms, sliced

1 red bell pepper, chopped

1 tablespoon olive oil

1 (16-ounce) jar Alfredo sauce

1 teaspoon dried thyme leaves

6 slices French bread

3 tablespoons butter, at room temperature

1. Preheat the air fryer by setting it to Roast and the temperature to 350°F.

2. In a medium bowl, combine the chicken, mushrooms, and bell pepper. Toss with the oil to coat. Arrange on the lowest rack of the air fryer.

3. Roast for 10 to 15 minutes, or until the chicken reaches an internal temperature of 165°F. Remove the food and place it in an 8-inch metal bowl. Stir in the Alfredo sauce and thyme. Return to the air fryer and roast for another 3 to 4 minutes until hot.

4. Meanwhile, spread the French bread slices with butter. When the chicken mixture is done, remove the bowl from the air fryer and set aside.

5. Place the bread slices on the rack. Toast for 2 to 4 minutes, or until golden brown.

6. Place the toast on a serving plate and top with the chicken to serve.

VARIATION TIP: Serve over hot mashed potatoes or hot cooked rice or even pasta. Toss the pasta with a bit of butter first.

*Pesto Bruschetta, page 43*

# CHAPTER FOUR

◆

# APPETIZERS AND SNACKS

# Steamed Pot Stickers

Makes **30 pot stickers** • DAIRY-FREE, VEGETARIAN

Setting: **Air Fry** • Temperature: **360°F** • Prep time: **20 minutes** • Cook time: **10 minutes**

*Pot stickers are little Chinese dumplings that you can fill with anything you want, although usually meat or vegetables are tucked inside. This vegetarian version is delicious. You can find wonton wrappers in the produce aisle of your supermarket.*

⅓ cup finely chopped cabbage

¼ cup finely chopped red bell pepper

2 scallions, white and green parts, diced

1 large egg, beaten

2 tablespoons cocktail sauce

2 teaspoons low-sodium soy sauce

30 wonton wrappers

½ cup water, divided

1. In a small bowl, combine the cabbage, bell pepper, scallions, egg, cocktail sauce, and soy sauce and mix well.

2. Place the wonton wrappers on a work surface. Put about 1 teaspoon of the filling mixture into the center of each wrapper. Fold the wrapper in half, covering the filling. Fill a small bowl with a few tablespoons of water. Dampen the edges of the wrapper with about ⅛ teaspoon of water and seal. You can crimp the edges with your fingers so they look like the pot stickers you get in restaurants. Brush each with another ⅛ teaspoon of water.

3. Carefully pour about ⅓ cup of water in the drip pan at the bottom of the air fryer.

4. Preheat the air fryer by setting it to Air Fry and the temperature to 360°F.

5. Arrange the pot stickers on the two oven racks and insert the racks into the bottom and middle holders. Air fry for 8 to 10 minutes, or until the pot stickers are hot and the bottoms are lightly browned.

# Pesto Bruschetta

Serves **4**

Setting: **Bake** • Temperature: **350°F** • Prep time: **10 minutes** • Cook time: **8 minutes**

*Pesto is a classic Italian sauce made with fresh basil, olive oil, garlic, pine nuts, and Parmesan cheese. Here, this sauce is mixed with fresh tomatoes and slathered onto warm, crisp cheese bread for a wonderful snack.*

8 slices (½ inch thick) French bread

2 tablespoons butter, at room temperature

1 cup shredded mozzarella cheese

1 cup chopped grape tomatoes

½ cup basil pesto

2 scallions, white and green parts, thinly sliced

1 tomato, sliced (optional)

Pine nuts, for garnish (optional)

1. Preheat the air fryer by setting it to Bake and the temperature to 350°F.

2. Spread the bread slices with the butter and place, butter-side up, on a rack. Insert the rack into the lower slots in the air fryer. Bake for 3 to 5 minutes, or until the bread is light golden brown.

3. Remove the bread from the air fryer and top each piece with some of the cheese. Return to the air fryer and bake for 1 to 3 minutes, or until the cheese melts.

4. Meanwhile, in a small bowl, stir together the tomatoes, pesto, and scallions.

5. When the cheese is melted, remove the bread from the air fryer and place on a serving plate. Top it with some of the pesto mixture and, if desired, an extra slice of tomato and crushed pine nuts for some crunch. Serve.

INGREDIENT TIP: You can find basil pesto and other types of pesto in the refrigerated section or the pasta aisle of any supermarket.

# Vegetable Egg Rolls

Makes **8 egg rolls** • DAIRY-FREE, VEGETARIAN

Setting: **Air Fry** • Temperature: **390°F** • Prep time: **15 minutes** • Cook time: **10 minutes**

*Egg rolls and the air fryer are a perfect match. The egg roll wrapping gets crisp and crunchy, and the interior is heated—all with very little oil. Enjoy these cute egg rolls with soy sauce or a purchased sweet-and-sour dipping sauce.*

½ cup chopped fresh mushrooms

½ cup grated carrot

½ cup chopped zucchini

2 scallions, white and green parts, minced

1 tablespoon low-sodium soy sauce

8 egg roll wrappers

1 tablespoon cornstarch

1 large egg, beaten

1. In a medium bowl, stir together the mushrooms, carrot, zucchini, scallions, and soy sauce.

2. Place the egg roll wrappers on a work surface. Top each with about 3 tablespoons of the vegetable mixture.

3. In a small bowl, whisk the cornstarch and egg well. Brush some of this mixture on the edges of the wrappers. Fold the sides of the wrappers in and over the filling and roll up the wrappers, enclosing the filling. Brush some of the egg mixture on the outside of the egg rolls to seal.

4. Preheat the air fryer by setting it to Air Fry and the temperature to 390°F.

5. Arrange the egg rolls on the two oven racks. Air fry for 7 to 10 minutes, or until the egg rolls are brown and crunchy.

VARIATION TIP: You can use spring roll wrappers in this recipe; they are thinner than egg roll wrappers and won't take as long to cook. Reduce the cooking time to 5 to 7 minutes if you choose this variation.

# Roasted Potatoes with Onion Dip

Serves **8** • GLUTEN-FREE, VEGETARIAN

Setting: **Air Fry, Rotate** • Temperature: **400°F** • Prep time: **10 minutes**

Cook time: **23 minutes**

*Tiny roasted potatoes make the perfect appetizer, especially when served with a creamy caramelized onion dip.*

1 pound creamer potatoes or tiny red potatoes

1 red, yellow, or white onion, chopped

4 teaspoons safflower oil

4 ounces cream cheese, at room temperature

¼ cup sour cream

¼ cup mayonnaise

2 teaspoons Worcestershire sauce

1 teaspoon dried thyme leaves

¼ teaspoon kosher salt

1. Rinse and dry the potatoes. In a large bowl, toss the potatoes with 2 teaspoons of oil to coat. In a small bowl, stir together the onion and remaining 2 teaspoons of oil to coat.

2. Preheat the air fryer by setting it to Air Fry and the temperature to 400°F.

3. Place the potatoes in the rotisserie basket and spread the onion evenly in the drip pan. Put the pan with the onion into the bottom of air fryer, then add the rotisserie basket using the rotisserie tool. Press Start and Rotate. If your air fryer does not have a rotisserie function, arrange the potatoes on a rack or in the air fryer basket and place the onion on the drip pan or a rimmed sheet pan.

4. Cook for 12 minutes, then check the onion. If brown and tender, remove it from the air fryer. Otherwise, let the onion cook for 2 to 3 minutes more. Once done, transfer the onion to a bowl to cool slightly.

5. In another small bowl, stir together the cream cheese, sour cream, mayonnaise, Worcestershire, thyme, and salt. Stir in the caramelized onion and transfer to a serving bowl. When the potatoes are crisp on the outside and easily pierced with a fork, 6 to 8 minutes more, place them in a serving bowl. Serve with the onion dip.

# Beef and Mango Skewers

Serves **4 to 6** • DAIRY-FREE, GLUTEN-FREE

Setting: **Air Fry** • Temperature: **390°F** • Prep time: **15 minutes** • Cook time: **7 minutes**

*Any kabob or skewer cooks beautifully in the air fryer. And this combination of tender smoky beef and sweet and juicy mango is spectacular. The meat develops a tender crust, and the fruit becomes caramelized. Make sure to use metal skewers, not wood, in the air fryer.*

1¼ pounds beef sirloin tip, cut into 1-inch cubes

3 tablespoons balsamic vinegar

1 tablespoon olive oil

1 tablespoon honey

½ teaspoon dried marjoram leaves

⅛ teaspoon kosher salt

Freshly ground black pepper

2 mangoes

1. In a medium bowl, combine the beef cubes, vinegar, oil, honey, marjoram, salt, and pepper to taste. Mix well, then massage the marinade into the beef with your hands. Set aside.

2. To prepare the mango, stand the fruit on end and cut off the skin using a sharp knife. Then carefully cut around the oval pit in the center to remove the flesh. Cut the mango into 1-inch cubes.

3. Thread the ingredients onto metal skewers, alternating 3 beef cubes with 2 mango cubes on each.

4. Preheat the air fryer by setting it to Air Fry and the temperature to 390°F.

5. Place the skewers on the two racks in the air fryer. Air fry to 4 to 7 minutes, or until the beef is browned and reaches an internal temperature of at least 145°F.

VARIATION TIP: Use peaches or nectarines in place of the mango if you can't find ripe mango. To test for ripeness, when pressed gently with your fingers, any stone fruit will give slightly and it will smell sweet.

# Arancini

Serves **4 to 6**

Setting: **Bake** • Temperature: **330°F** • Prep time: **18 minutes** • Cook time: **12 minutes**

*Arancini are little rice balls that are a popular Italian appetizer. The rice is stuffed with cheese, then deep-fried, making an irresistible snack. You need to use firm block mozzarella cheese for this recipe, not the type sold packed in water.*

2 cups cooked, cooled rice or leftover rice, cooled

2 large eggs, beaten

1½ cups panko breadcrumbs, divided

½ cup grated Parmesan cheese

2 tablespoons minced fresh basil leaves

4 ounces mozzarella cheese, cut into ¾-inch cubes

2 tablespoons olive oil

1. In a medium bowl, combine the rice, eggs, ½ cup of breadcrumbs, Parmesan cheese, and basil and mix gently. Form the rice mixture into 16 (1½-inch) balls.

2. Poke a hole in each ball with your finger and insert a cheese cube. Form the rice mixture firmly around the cheese.

3. On a shallow plate, combine the remaining 1 cup of breadcrumbs with the oil and mix well. Roll the rice balls in the breadcrumb mixture to coat.

4. Preheat the air fryer by setting it to Bake and the temperature to 330°F.

5. Place the arancini on the wire racks and place the racks on the middle and bottom slots in the air fryer. Bake for 8 to 12 minutes, or until golden brown.

VARIATION TIP: Serve these little arancini with a dipping sauce made of pasta sauce with more herbs stirred in or make a sauce of mustard and sour cream or mayonnaise.

# Spicy Beef Jerky Dip

Serves **4**

Setting: **Dehydrate** • Temperature: **160°F**

Prep time: **15 minutes, plus 1 hour 45 minutes to freeze and marinate, plus 2 hours to chill for serving** • Cook time: **3 hours 30 minutes**

*Beef jerky adds a smoky, spicy note to this appetizer dip. Serve with cherry tomatoes, bell peppers, zucchini, carrots, and summer squash.*

1 pound lean beef steak (such as flank or tri-tip), trimmed of visible fat

¼ cup low-sodium soy sauce

3 tablespoons lime juice, divided

½ teaspoon red pepper flakes

½ cup sour cream

⅓ cup mayonnaise

1 tablespoon spicy brown mustard

1 scallion, white and green parts, minced

1. Freeze the beef for 45 minutes to make slicing it easier.

2. Meanwhile, in a medium bowl, stir together the soy sauce, 2 tablespoons of lime juice, and red pepper flakes.

3. Thinly slice the beef against the grain. In a shallow glass pan, combine the beef and soy sauce mixture. Cover and refrigerator for 1 hour.

4. Drain the marinade and pat the beef dry with paper towels. Place the beef in a single layer, without overlapping, on the two cooking racks.

5. Insert the drip pan in the bottom of the cooking chamber and insert the racks; one in the top position and the other in the middle.

6. Select Dehydrate and adjust the temperature to 160°F. Set the timer for 3 hours.

7. After 1½ hours, switch the racks.

8. When cooking is almost complete, test a piece of jerky by bending it at a 90-degree angle. If any moisture seeps out, dehydrate for 20 to 30 minutes more. When done, remove and cool. Dice enough jerky to make ½ cup.

9. In a small bowl, stir together the sour cream, mayonnaise, the remaining 1 tablespoon of lime juice, mustard, and scallion. Stir in the diced jerky. Cover and refrigerate for a few hours before serving.

VARIATION TIP: Store the remaining jerky for up to 2 months in an airtight container at room temperature.

# Hash Brown Bruschetta

Serves **4 to 6** • GLUTEN-FREE

Setting: **Air Fry** • Temperature: **400°F** • Prep time: **8 minutes** • Cook time: **10 minutes**

*Bruschetta is usually made of crisp toast piled with ingredients such as chopped tomatoes and herbs. In this recipe, crisp hash brown potatoes stand in for the toast for a gluten-free version. Frozen hash brown potatoes crisp up in the air fryer with very little fat and become deliciously crunchy.*

6 frozen hash brown potato patties

½ cup chopped cherry tomatoes

⅓ cup diced Provolone cheese

¼ cup grated Parmesan cheese

2 tablespoons balsamic vinegar

1 tablespoon olive oil

1 tablespoon minced fresh basil leaves

1. Preheat the air fryer by setting it to Air Fry and the temperature to 400°F.

2. Arrange the hash brown patties on the air fryer racks in a single layer. Air fry for 7 to 10 minutes, or until the potatoes are crisp, hot, and golden brown.

3. Meanwhile, in a small bowl, stir together the cherry tomatoes, Provolone cheese, Parmesan cheese, vinegar, oil, and basil.

4. When the potatoes are done, carefully remove from the air fryer and arrange on a serving plate. Top with the tomato mixture and serve.

INGREDIENT TIP: Make sure to buy hash brown patties, not the loose variety, since they form the base that holds the tomato mixture.

# Sweet and Hot Chicken Wings

Serves **4 to 6** • DAIRY-FREE, GLUTEN-FREE

Setting: **Bake** • Temperature: **390°F** • Prep time: **10 minutes** • Cook time: **25 minutes**

*The air fryer makes great chicken wings that are crisp and tender. The sweet and hot sauce is the perfect finishing touch for this easy appetizer.*

10 whole chicken wings

1 tablespoon olive oil

½ cup packed brown sugar

3 tablespoons honey

½ cup apple cider vinegar

3 garlic cloves, minced

½ teaspoon red pepper flakes

½ teaspoon salt

INGREDIENT TIP: You can sometimes find chicken "drumettes" in the meat section of the supermarket. They are made from the large section of the chicken wing and really do look like little drumsticks. If you want to use these instead of the cut-up whole wings, use about 14 in this recipe.

1. Cut each chicken wing into 3 pieces. You'll have one large piece, one medium piece, and one small end. Discard the small end or save it for stock.

2. In a medium bowl, toss the wings with the oil to coat. Arrange the wings on two racks.

3. Preheat the air fryer by setting it to Bake and the temperature to 390°F.

4. Put the racks into the air fryer and bake for 18 minutes, turning the wings over halfway through the cooking time.

5. Meanwhile, in a small bowl, stir together the brown sugar, honey, vinegar, garlic, red pepper flakes, and salt.

6. Remove the wings from the air fryer and put them into a 7-inch round pan. Pour the sauce over the wings and toss to coat.

7. Put the pan into the air fryer on the lower level and cook for 5 to 7 minutes, or until the wings register 165°F on a food thermometer and are glazed.

*Crispy French Fries,*
*page 56*

# CHAPTER FIVE

···· ✦ ····

# VEGETABLES AND SIDES

# Roasted Bell Peppers with Garlic

Serves **4 to 6** • DAIRY-FREE, GLUTEN-FREE, VEGAN

Setting: **Roast** • Temperature: **350°F** • Prep time: **15 minutes** • Cook time: **26 minutes**

*A mixture of colorful roasted bell peppers is not only beautiful—it's also good for you. The garlic adds a sweet and nutty note, and the cloves get very tender and sticky when roasted. Serve this easy side dish with a meat loaf or roasted chicken for a great meal.*

2 red bell peppers, sliced into 1-inch strips

1 yellow bell pepper, sliced into 1-inch strips

1 orange bell pepper, sliced into 1-inch strips

1 green bell pepper, sliced into 1-inch strips

2 tablespoons olive oil, divided, plus more for coating the foil square

1 teaspoon dried marjoram leaves

⅛ teaspoon kosher salt

Freshly ground black pepper

1 head garlic

1. In a large bowl, toss the red, yellow, orange, and green pepper strips with 1 tablespoon of oil to coat. Sprinkle with the marjoram, salt, and pepper to taste and toss again.

2. Cut off the top of the garlic head to expose the cloves and place it, cut-side up, on an oiled square of aluminum foil. Drizzle with the remaining 1 tablespoon of oil and wrap the garlic loosely in the foil.

3. Preheat the air fryer by setting it to Roast and the temperature to 350°F.

4. Place the wrapped garlic on the lower rack in the air fryer. Roast for 18 minutes, then add the pepper strips to the air fryer, some to the lower rack and some to the upper rack, in a single layer. Roast for 5 to 8 minutes, or until the peppers are tender and the garlic is soft. Transfer to a serving plate.

5. Remove the garlic from the air fryer and unwrap it. Using a hot pad, carefully squeeze the cloves out of their paper skins and mix with the bell peppers to serve.

# Roasted Brussels Sprouts

Serves **4 to 6** • GLUTEN-FREE

Setting: **Roast** • Temperature: **370°F** • Prep time: **10 minutes** • Cook time: **26 minutes**

*Many people (including me!) don't like Brussels sprouts because they can be bitter. But when this cruciferous vegetable is roasted until golden and crisp, the mini cabbages become tender and sweet. Serve with Bacon-Mustard Rotisserie Chicken (page 82) for a hearty dinner.*

1½ pounds Brussels
  sprouts
2 tablespoons olive oil
1 tablespoon lemon juice
½ teaspoon kosher salt
⅛ teaspoon freshly
  ground black pepper
⅓ cup grated Parmesan
  cheese

1. Preheat the air fryer by setting it to Roast and the temperature to 370°F.

2. Trim the bottoms from the Brussels sprouts and pull off any discolored leaves. Place them in a large bowl and toss with the oil, lemon juice, salt, and pepper to coat. Arrange in a single layer on the air fryer racks.

3. Roast for 20 minutes, then check. When the sprouts are dark golden brown and crisp, they are done. You may need to roast for 5 to 6 minutes more.

4. Transfer the Brussels sprouts to a serving dish and toss with the Parmesan cheese.

VARIATION TIP: Use cauliflower florets instead of Brussels sprouts. Just make sure that the florets are all about the same size so they roast evenly. Roast for 15 to 18 minutes, or until light golden brown and tender, then toss with the Parmesan.

# Crispy French Fries

Serves **4 to 6** • GLUTEN-FREE, VEGETARIAN

Setting: **Air Fry, Rotate** • Temperature: **390°F** • Prep time: **5 minutes**

Cook time: **18 minutes**

*What's better than super-crisp French fries? This classic recipe is simple and delicious. If you use thicker frozen French fries, increase the cooking time by about 5 minutes.*

6 cups frozen thin or
   thick French fries
1 tablespoon olive oil
½ teaspoon kosher salt

1. Remove any ice on the French fries. In a large bowl, toss the French fries with the oil to coat, then place them in the rotisserie basket.

2. Preheat the air fryer by setting it to Air Fry and the temperature to 390°F.

3. Put the basket in place using the rotisserie tool. Set the timer to 10 minutes and press Start and Rotate. If your air fryer does not have a rotisserie function, arrange the potatoes on a rack or in the air fryer basket.

4. Air fry for 16 to 18 minutes, or until the fries are golden brown and hot.

5. Put the fries in a serving bowl, sprinkle with salt, and serve hot with your favorite dipping sauce.

VARIATION TIP: You can use raw potatoes in this recipe; choose russets for best results. Peel the potatoes and cut into ¼-inch strips. Pat them dry with paper towels before adding to the rotisserie basket. Add 2 to 5 minutes to the cook time. Mix them with ½ cup Parmesan cheese and some dried thyme and basil leaves for a flavor boost!

# Cream Cheese Buns

Serves **6** • VEGETARIAN

Setting: **Bake** • Temperature: **380°F** • Prep time: **15 minutes** • Cook time: **10 minutes**

*This wonderful and unusual recipe uses garlic-flavored cream cheese as the filling for crisp, golden buns. Serve the buns alongside a green salad tossed with chickpeas, bell peppers, and sunflower seeds for a delicious lunch.*

6 (3- to 4-inch) round hard buns

1 (8-ounce) package cream cheese, at room temperature

2 tablespoons heavy (whipping) cream

½ teaspoon garlic powder

6 tablespoons (¾ stick) butter

3 garlic cloves, minced

1 teaspoon dried thyme leaves

½ teaspoon kosher salt

1. Carefully slice the buns into four equal wedges, but do not slice all the way through them.

2. In a medium bowl, stir together the cream cheese, heavy cream, and garlic powder until well mixed. Spoon or pipe this mixture into the cuts in the buns, being careful not to break them apart. Gently press the buns back into shape.

3. In a small saucepan over medium-low heat, combine the butter, garlic, and thyme. Cook for about 2 minutes until the butter sizzles and the garlic is fragrant.

4. Preheat the air fryer by setting it to Bake and the temperature to 380°F.

5. Place the buns carefully on one or two rimmed sheet pans. Drizzle each bun with some of the garlic butter mixture and sprinkle with salt.

6. Bake for 5 to 8 minutes, or until the cream cheese is melted and the buns are golden brown. Let cool for 5 minutes and serve.

INGREDIENT TIP: Use brown-and-serve rolls in this recipe if you'd like. Just prepare them according to the package instructions, let them cool, and proceed with the recipe.

# Creamy Corn Casserole

Serves **4 to 6** • VEGETARIAN

Setting: **Bake** • Temperature: **320°F** • Prep time: **7 minutes** • Cook time: **18 minutes**

*An old-fashioned casserole is comforting and homey, and the perfect side for any main—from roasted chicken to meat loaf. As a bonus, kids love it, too! The cheese adds flavor and great texture to this delicious recipe.*

Nonstick cooking spray

¼ cup all-purpose flour

1 large egg, beaten

⅓ cup whole milk

½ cup light cream

¼ teaspoon kosher salt

Freshly ground black pepper

3 cups frozen corn, not thawed

1 cup grated Swiss or Havarti cheese

3 tablespoons butter, cut into cubes

1. Preheat the air fryer by setting it to Bake and the temperature to 320°F.

2. Coat a 7-inch baking pan with cooking spray.

3. In a medium bowl, whisk the flour, egg, milk, cream, salt, and pepper to taste until combined. Add the corn and cheese and whisk to combine. Pour the mixture into the prepared pan and dot it with the butter.

4. Bake for 15 to 18 minutes, or until the casserole is set and puffed.

VARIATION TIP: Use canned corn in place of the frozen corn in this recipe; just drain it well. You'll need 2 (15-ounce) cans of corn, drained, to make 3 cups.

# Potato Vegetable Salad

Serves **4 to 6** • DAIRY-FREE, GLUTEN-FREE, VEGAN

Setting: **Air Fry, Rotate** • Temperature: **350°F**

Prep time: **10 minutes, plus 3 hours to chill (optional)** • Cook time: **25 minutes**

*Potato salad is a versatile dish you can serve any time of the year. This recipe is easy to make with small red or creamer potatoes. The hot potatoes will soak up the lemony dressing for a well-flavored salad.*

2 pounds creamer potatoes or tiny red potatoes, halved

1 tablespoon olive oil, plus ⅓ cup

⅛ teaspoon kosher salt

Freshly ground black pepper

1 red bell pepper, chopped

2 scallions, white and green parts, chopped

⅓ cup lemon juice

3 tablespoons Dijon or yellow mustard

VARIATION TIP: Add fresh basil leaves, chives, or rosemary with the bell pepper and dressing. The warmth of the potatoes will deepen the flavor of the herbs.

1. In a large bowl, toss the potatoes with 1 tablespoon of oil to coat.

2. Preheat the air fryer by setting it to Air Fry and the temperature to 350°F.

3. Put the potatoes in the rotisserie basket and put the basket into the air fryer using the rotisserie tool.

4. Set the timer for 25 minutes, then press Start and Rotate. If your air fryer does not have a rotisserie function, arrange the potatoes on a rack or in the air fryer basket.

5. Meanwhile, place the bell pepper and scallions in a large bowl.

6. In a small bowl, combine the remaining ⅓ cup of oil, the lemon juice, and mustard and whisk well.

7. When the potatoes are cooked, add them to the bowl with the bell pepper and scallions and drizzle with the dressing. Toss gently.

8. Let the salad cool for 20 minutes. Stir gently and serve warm, or refrigerate for 2 to 3 hours and serve chilled.

# Scalloped Potatoes

Serves **4 to 6** • GLUTEN-FREE, VEGETARIAN

Setting: **Bake** • Temperature: **380°F** • Prep time: **12 minutes** • Cook time: **20 minutes**

*Rich scalloped potatoes cook to perfection in the air fryer and only require a few ingredients. You can substitute half-and-half or whole milk for the heavy cream, but the dish will be less rich. You could use frozen diced potatoes; just thaw them before using in the recipe.*

Nonstick cooking spray

3 cups refrigerated diced potatoes

¾ cup heavy (whipping) cream

3 garlic cloves, minced

¼ teaspoon kosher salt

Freshly ground black pepper

1. Preheat the air fryer by setting it to Bake and the temperature to 380°F.

2. Coat a 7-inch round pan with cooking spray. In the prepared pan, stir together the potatoes, heavy cream, garlic, salt, and pepper to taste; arrange the potatoes in an even layer.

3. Bake for 15 to 20 minutes, or until the potatoes are golden brown on top and tender.

VARIATION TIP: Add some shredded cheese to these potatoes. Use about ⅔ cup of Gouda, Havarti, or Provolone for a delicious twist. Scalloped potatoes made with cheese are called au gratin.

# Garlic and Sesame Carrots

Serves **4 to 6** • DAIRY-FREE, GLUTEN-FREE, VEGAN

Setting: **Air Fry, Rotate** • Temperature: **380°F** • Prep time: **5 minutes**

Cook time: **16 minutes**

*Kids tend to love carrots, but adults often consider them kind of boring. Not this recipe! The air fryer intensifies the sweetness of the carrots and the texture is superb. The sesame seeds add flavor and crunch.*

1 pound baby carrots

1 tablespoon sesame oil

½ teaspoon dried dill weed

⅛ teaspoon kosher salt

Freshly ground black pepper

6 garlic cloves, peeled

3 tablespoons sesame seeds

1. In a large bowl, toss the carrots with the oil, dill, salt, and pepper to taste.

2. Preheat the air fryer by setting it to Air Fry and the temperature to 380°F.

3. Arrange the carrots in the rotisserie basket. Put the basket in place using the rotisserie tool. Press Start and Rotate. Cook for 8 minutes. Remove the basket, open it, and add the garlic. Close the basket and return it to the air fryer. Roast for 6 to 8 minutes more, or until the garlic and carrots are lightly browned. If your air fryer does not have a rotisserie function, place the carrots in a single layer on one or two racks. Air fry for 10 to 14 minutes, or until the carrots and garlic are lightly browned.

4. Transfer to a serving bowl, sprinkle with the sesame seeds, and serve.

INGREDIENT TIP: Toast the sesame seeds for more flavor, but don't use the air fryer because they will blow around in the moving air. Toast the seeds in a dry pan over low heat on the stovetop for 2 to 4 minutes until they are light golden and fragrant.

# Herbed Vegetable Mélange

Serves **4 to 6** • DAIRY-FREE, GLUTEN-FREE, VEGAN

Setting: **Roast** • Temperature: **350°F** • Prep time: **15 minutes** • Cook time: **18 minutes**

*Roasted vegetables complement just about any meal, whether you are serving a grilled steak, roasted chicken, or hamburgers. Choose tender vegetables, not root vegetables like carrots, for this recipe; that way, they will all roast at the same time and be delicious and crisp-tender.*

1 red bell pepper, sliced

1 yellow bell pepper, sliced

1 orange bell pepper, sliced

1 (8-ounce) package sliced button mushrooms

1 yellow summer squash, sliced

5 garlic cloves, sliced

2 tablespoons olive oil

1 tablespoon lemon juice

1 teaspoon dried thyme leaves

½ teaspoon dried basil leaves

1. Preheat the air fryer by setting it to Roast and the temperature to 350°F.

2. In a large bowl, combine the bell peppers, mushrooms, squash, garlic, oil, lemon juice, thyme, and basil. Toss to coat. Arrange the vegetables on the air fryer racks.

3. Roast for 14 to 18 minutes, or until the vegetables are tender.

VARIATION TIP: Vary the herbs in this recipe, or use spices like smoked paprika, cumin, or chili powder. Or add some low-sodium soy sauce and ground ginger for an exotic twist.

*Fish and Chips, page* 73

# CHAPTER SIX

✦

# FISH AND SEAFOOD

# Seafood Tacos

Serves **4 to 6**

Setting: **Air Fry** • Temperature: **400°F** • Prep time: **15 minutes** • Cook time: **12 minutes**

*Seafood tacos are a popular street food in California, where fresh fish is caught every day. This easy recipe is full of flavor and perfect for a warm summer evening. You just put everything on the table and let each person assemble their own creation.*

1½ pounds white fish fillets (such as snapper)

2 tablespoons olive oil

3 tablespoons lemon juice, divided

2 cups chopped cabbage

1 yellow bell pepper, shredded or chopped

¾ cup salsa

8 soft taco-size flour tortillas

⅔ cup sour cream

1 tomato, chopped (optional)

2 avocados, peeled, pitted, and chopped (optional)

1. Preheat the air fryer by setting it to Air Fry and the temperature to 400°F.

2. Brush the fish with the oil and sprinkle with 1 tablespoon of lemon juice. Arrange the fish in a single layer on one or two of the air fryer racks. Air fry for 9 to 12 minutes, or until the fish just flakes when tested with a fork.

3. Meanwhile, in a medium bowl, stir together the cabbage, bell pepper, remaining 2 tablespoons of lemon juice, and salsa.

4. When the fish is done, remove it from the air fryer and break into pieces. Let everyone assemble their own tacos by topping off tortillas with the fish, cabbage mixture, sour cream, and chopped tomatoes and avocado (if using).

VARIATION TIP: Use scallops, shrimp, lobster tails, or a combination of your favorite seafood in this recipe. And you can add cheese to the tacos; try shredded pepper Jack or Monterey Jack.

# Crab Ratatouille

Serves **4 to 6** • DAIRY-FREE, GLUTEN-FREE

Setting: **Roast** • Temperature: **400°F** • Prep time: **15 minutes** • Cook time: **15 minutes**

*Ratatouille is a French dish that is made from eggplant, tomatoes, and veggies, usually stewed for hours until the vegetables are tender. This fresh version adds crab for a heartier meal and is made in a fraction of the time in the air fryer.*

2 cups cubed peeled eggplant

1 onion, chopped

1 red bell pepper, chopped

2 large tomatoes, chopped

2 tablespoons olive oil

1 teaspoon dried thyme leaves

½ teaspoon dried basil leaves

¼ teaspoon kosher salt

Freshly ground black pepper

2 cups cooked crabmeat, picked over

1. Preheat the air fryer by setting it to Roast and the temperature to 400°F.

2. In an 8-inch metal bowl, combine the eggplant, onion, bell pepper, tomatoes, oil, thyme, basil, salt, and pepper to taste and mix gently.

3. Roast for 10 minutes, then remove the bowl from the air fryer and stir.

4. Add the crabmeat and roast for 3 to 5 minutes, or until the ratatouille is bubbling and the vegetables are tender.

INGREDIENT TIP: You can buy crabmeat in a can, or you can often find tubs of shelled cooked crab at the fish counter in many supermarkets. Pick it over carefully to remove any cartilage or shells before proceeding with the recipe.

# Crispy Herbed Salmon

Serves **4 to 6** • DAIRY-FREE

Setting: **Bake** • Temperature: **320°F** • Prep time: **10 minutes** • Cook time: **13 minutes**

*Healthy salmon is a great fish for air frying. In this recipe, the crisp topping made of potato chips and breadcrumbs contrasts perfectly with the tender, moist fish. The honey mustard and lemon juice add great flavor. Serve with some roasted broccoli or fresh fruit.*

6 (6-ounce) skinless
   salmon fillets

¼ cup honey mustard

1 tablespoon lemon juice

1 teaspoon dried thyme
   leaves

½ cup crushed potato
   chips

⅓ cup panko
   breadcrumbs

2 tablespoons olive oil

1. Preheat the air fryer by setting it to Bake and the temperature to 320°F.

2. Place the salmon on two plates. In a small bowl, stir together the mustard, lemon juice, and thyme and spread the mixture evenly on the salmon.

3. In another small bowl, combine the potato chips and breadcrumbs and mix well. Add the oil and mix until combined.

4. Arrange the salmon in a single layer on one or two air fryer racks and press the breadcrumb mixture, gently but firmly, onto each fillet. Fit the racks into the air fryer.

5. Bake for 9 to 13 minutes, or until the internal temperature of the salmon reaches at least 145°F and the topping is browned and crisp.

INGREDIENT TIP: Panko breadcrumbs are different from regular dried breadcrumbs. They have tiny points on each crumb that make an exceptionally crisp topping. You can find them in the grocery store next to the regular breadcrumbs.

# Shrimp and Peppers

Serves **4 to 6** • DAIRY-FREE, GLUTEN-FREE

Setting: **Air Fry, Rotate** • Temperature: **400°F** • Prep time: **15 minutes**

Cook time: **11 minutes**

*If you love the classic Italian sausage and peppers, you will love shrimp and peppers! Chopped fresh tomatoes are added at the end for a sweet note. Serve this dish in a bowl with toasted French bread for dipping.*

1 pound raw large shrimp, shelled and deveined

1 red bell pepper, sliced

1 yellow bell pepper, sliced

2 tablespoons olive oil

1 teaspoon dried Italian seasoning

½ teaspoon kosher salt

1 red onion, thinly sliced

1 cup chopped beefsteak tomato

2 tablespoons dry white wine (optional)

1. Preheat the air fryer by setting it to Air Fry and the temperature to 400°F.

2. In a large bowl, combine the shrimp and red and yellow bell peppers; drizzle with the oil and sprinkle with Italian seasoning and salt; toss to coat. Place the shrimp, bell peppers, and onion in the rotisserie basket.

3. Insert the basket using the rotisserie tool. Press Start and Rotate and cook for 8 to 11 minutes. If your air fryer does not have a rotisserie function, arrange the shrimp and vegetables on a rack, or in the air fryer basket.

4. Meanwhile, in a serving bowl, stir together the tomatoes and wine (if using).

5. When the shrimp are pink and the peppers and onion are tender, remove from the air fryer and add to the tomatoes in the serving bowl. Stir gently and serve.

INGREDIENT TIP: Shrimp are sold by the number of shrimp in a pound. The larger the shrimp, the smaller the count. For instance, for this recipe you should choose large shrimp that would be 31 to 35 shrimp per pound. Medium shrimp would be 41 to 50 per pound.

# Tuna Veggie Stir-Fry

Serves **4 to 6** • DAIRY-FREE

Setting: **Air Fry** • Temperature: **380°F** • Prep time: **15 minutes** • Cook time: **13 minutes**

*It's easy to make stir-fry recipes in the air fryer. You just don't have to stir it much! This family-friendly recipe is hearty and simple and can be on the table in less than 30 minutes. Serve over hot cooked rice.*

1 red bell pepper, chopped

1 cup green beans, cut into 2-inch pieces

1 onion, thinly sliced

1 tablespoon olive oil

3 garlic cloves, sliced

3 tablespoons low-sodium soy sauce

2 tablespoons honey

1 pound fresh raw tuna, cubed

1. Preheat the air fryer by setting it to Air Fry and the temperature to 380°F.

2. In an 8-inch metal bowl, stir together the bell pepper, green beans, onion, oil, and garlic. Air fry for 4 to 6 minutes, stirring once, until the vegetables are crisp-tender.

3. Stir in the soy sauce, honey, and tuna.

4. Cook for 3 to 7 minutes, stirring once, until the tuna is cooked as desired. You can cook it to rare, medium-rare, or well done.

INGREDIENT TIP: Fresh tuna can be served rare, and some people prefer it that way. Cook it to the doneness you prefer. When you buy tuna at the store, ask for sushi grade for food-safety reasons.

# Scallops and Spring Veggies

Serves **4 to 6** • DAIRY-FREE, GLUTEN-FREE

Setting: **Roast** • Temperature: **400°F** • Prep time: **12 minutes** • Cook time: **11 minutes**

*Scallops are sweet and tender and cook in minutes, which makes them ideal for a quick dinner. When paired with fresh spring vegetables, they make an elegant meal. The veggies are flavored simply with lemon juice, thyme, and salt.*

12 ounces asparagus, ends trimmed, cut into 2-inch pieces

1½ cups sugar snap peas

1½ pounds sea scallops

2 tablespoons lemon juice

1 tablespoon olive oil

1 teaspoon dried thyme leaves

¼ teaspoon kosher salt

Freshly ground black pepper

1. Preheat the air fryer by setting it to Roast and the temperature to 400°F.

2. Arrange the asparagus and sugar snap peas on one rack. Place the rack in the lower part of the air fryer. Roast for 2 to 3 minutes, or until the vegetables are just becoming tender.

3. Meanwhile, check the scallops to see if they have a small muscle attached to the side. If they do, pull it off and discard it because that muscle will be tough when cooked.

4. In a medium bowl, toss the scallops with the lemon juice, oil, thyme, salt, and pepper to taste and arrange them on the second air fryer rack. Put the rack into the upper part of the air fryer.

5. Roast for 5 to 8 minutes until the scallops are firm when tested with your finger and are opaque in the center and the vegetables are tender.

   INGREDIENT TIP: Sea scallops are larger than bay scallops. Here's an easy way to remember this: A sea is larger than a bay. Scallops should smell sweet and of the ocean when they are raw.

# Snapper Scampi

Serves **4 to 6** • GLUTEN-FREE

Setting: **Air Fry** • Temperature: **390°F** • Prep time: **5 minutes** • Cook time: **10 minutes**

*"Scampi" means two things: large shrimp, or a dish that combines shrimp with lemon and garlic. Here, you'll swap the shrimp for red snapper or arctic char fillets for a simple, delicious dish. The lemon and garlic add great flavor.*

6 (6-ounce) skinless red snapper or arctic char fillets

2 tablespoons olive oil

4 tablespoons freshly squeezed lemon juice, divided

1 teaspoon dried basil leaves

¼ teaspoon kosher salt

3 tablespoons butter

3 garlic cloves, minced

½ teaspoon grated lemon zest

1. Preheat the air fryer by setting it to Air Fry and the temperature to 390°F.

2. Drizzle the fish with the oil and 1 tablespoon of lemon juice. Sprinkle with basil and salt and arrange in a single layer on the air fryer rack or racks.

3. Air fry for 7 to 8 minutes, or until the fish just flakes with a fork.

4. Put the fish on a serving plate and cover to keep warm.

5. In a 6-inch baking pan, combine the butter, remaining 3 tablespoons of lemon juice, garlic, and lemon zest and place in the air fryer. Air fry for 1 to 2 minutes, or until the garlic is sizzling. Pour the sauce over the fish and serve.

INGREDIENT TIP: Bottled lemon juice works for many recipes, but for a recipe like this one, where there are few ingredients and the flavor is so important, squeeze the juice from a fresh lemon. You can use a rasp grater or a lemon zester to get the lemon zest. To get the most juice out of a lemon, roll it on the counter first to break up the fruit a bit.

# Fish and Chips

Serves **4** • DAIRY-FREE, GLUTEN-FREE

Setting: **Air Fry, Rotate** • Temperature: **380°F** • Prep time: **10 minutes**

Cook time: **20 minutes**

*In British vernacular, "chips" means French fries. This classic recipe is easy to make in an air fryer using the rotisserie basket and a baking sheet.*

4 (6-ounce) fish fillets (tilapia, red snapper, or cod)

½ teaspoon dried marjoram leaves

¼ teaspoon kosher salt

Freshly ground black pepper

1 large egg white

¾ cup crushed potato chips

1 tablespoon olive oil

5 cups frozen French fries

Tartar sauce, for serving

INGREDIENT TIP: You can buy tartar sauce or make your own: In a small bowl, stir together ½ cup mayonnaise, 3 tablespoons chopped sweet pickle, 1 tablespoon lemon juice, and 1 tablespoon chopped fresh parsley.

1. Pat the fish fillets dry with paper towel and sprinkle with the marjoram, salt, and pepper to taste. Set aside.

2. In a shallow bowl, beat the egg white until foamy. In another shallow bowl, stir together the potato chips and oil.

3. Dip the tops of the fish into the egg white, then into the potato chip mixture, pressing firmly. Place the fish, potato chip–side up, on a baking sheet.

4. Preheat the air fryer by setting it to Air Fry and the temperature to 380°F.

5. Put the French fries into the rotisserie basket and put the basket into the air fryer. Set the timer for 14 minutes, and press Start and Rotate. If your air fryer does not have a rotisserie function, arrange the fries on one rack, or in the air fryer basket, and the fish on another rack. Cook the fish and fries separately if you have a basket-type air fryer.

6. When the timer goes off, place the baking sheet with the fish into the bottom of the air fryer. Close the door, set the timer for 6 minutes and press Start and Rotate.

7. Cook until the fish flakes and the fries are golden brown. Serve hot with tartar sauce.

*Sweet-and-Sour Drumsticks*
*page* 78

## CHAPTER SEVEN

✦

# POULTRY

# Roasted Veggie Chicken Salad

Serves **4 to 6** • DAIRY-FREE, GLUTEN-FREE

Setting: **Roast** • Temperature: **400°F** • Prep time: **12 minutes** • Cook time: **15 minutes**

*Have you ever eaten warm chicken salad? It has more flavor than chicken salad served cold and is quicker to prepare. This salad is full of colorful and nutritious ingredients for a great lunch or dinner.*

4 boneless, skinless chicken breasts, cut into 1-inch pieces

½ cup honey mustard salad dressing, divided

1 teaspoon dried thyme leaves

1 red onion, sliced

1 orange bell pepper, sliced

1 cup sliced zucchini

1 cup sliced yellow summer squash

½ cup mayonnaise

2 tablespoons lemon juice

Lettuce leaves, for serving (optional)

1. Preheat the air fryer by setting it to Roast and the temperature to 400°F.

2. Arrange the chicken on one air fryer rack. Drizzle with ¼ cup of honey mustard dressing and sprinkle with the thyme. Arrange the onion, bell pepper, zucchini, and summer squash on the second rack.

3. Put the rack with the chicken into the upper part of the air fryer and the rack with the vegetables into the lower part of the air fryer.

4. Roast for 10 to 15 minutes, or until the chicken reaches 165°F and the vegetables are tender.

5. Meanwhile, in a serving bowl, stir together the remaining ¼ cup of honey mustard dressing, the mayonnaise, and the lemon juice.

6. When the food is done, add it to the dressing mixture in the bowl and stir gently. Serve on lettuce leaves (if using).

VARIATION TIP: You can chill this salad in the fridge and use it as filling for sandwiches. Cover and chill for 3 to 4 hours. Choose croissants, pita bread, or ciabatta rolls to hold the filling.

# Chinese-Inspired Turkey Meatballs

Serves **4 to 6** • DAIRY-FREE

Setting: **Bake** • Temperature: **400°F** • Prep time: **15 minutes** • Cook time: **18 minutes**

*Asian flavors make turkey meatballs sing. To make the most tender meatballs, combine all the other ingredients and add the ground turkey last; mix gently and don't handle the mixture too much.*

1 onion, minced

2 tablespoons peanut oil or safflower oil, divided

⅓ cup finely chopped water chestnuts

⅓ cup panko breadcrumbs

3 tablespoons low-sodium soy sauce

½ teaspoon ground ginger

1 large egg, beaten

1¼ pounds ground turkey

1. Preheat the air fryer by setting it to Bake and the temperature to 400°F.

2. On a rimmed sheet pan, toss the onion with 1 tablespoon of oil. Cook for 2 to 3 minutes or until crisp-tender; transfer the onion to a medium bowl.

3. Add the water chestnuts, breadcrumbs, soy sauce, ginger, and egg to the onion and mix well. Stir in the ground turkey just until combined. Form the mixture into 1¼-inch meatballs. Arrange the meatballs on the sheet pan and drizzle with the remaining 1 tablespoon of oil.
You may need to cook in batches depending on the size of your air fryer.

4. Bake for 10 to 15 minutes, or until the internal temperature of the meatballs reaches 165°F.

VARIATION TIP: Add a sauce. In an 8-inch metal bowl, whisk 2 tablespoons cornstarch, ¾ cup chicken broth, and ⅓ cup pineapple juice to blend. When the meatballs are done, pour the sauce over them and cook for 4 to 5 minutes, or until the sauce thickens. Serve over rice.

# Sweet-and-Sour Drumsticks

Serves **4 to 6** • DAIRY-FREE, GLUTEN-FREE

Setting: **Bake** • Temperature: **350°F** • Prep time: **5 minutes** • Cook time: **25 minutes**

*Cooking chicken drumsticks in the air fryer is a two-part process. The meat is first cooked until done, then coated with a sweet-and-sour sauce and cooked until glazed. This extra step creates a crisp and delicious coating.*

6 chicken drumsticks

3 tablespoons lemon juice, divided

3 tablespoons low-sodium soy sauce, divided

1 tablespoon peanut oil or safflower oil

3 tablespoons honey

3 tablespoons brown sugar

2 tablespoons ketchup

¼ cup pineapple juice

1. Preheat the air fryer by setting it to Bake and the temperature to 350°F.

2. Sprinkle the drumsticks with 1 tablespoon of lemon juice, 1 tablespoon of soy sauce, and the oil. Place on a rack and insert into the lower slots in the air fryer. Bake for 18 minutes, or until the internal temperature of the drumsticks is about 155°F.

3. Meanwhile, in a 7-inch bowl, stir together the remaining 2 tablespoons of lemon juice, remaining 2 tablespoons of soy sauce, the honey, brown sugar, ketchup, and pineapple juice.

4. Add the drumsticks to the bowl and stir to coat well with the sauce.

5. Place the bowl on the air fryer rack. Bake for 5 to 7 minutes, or until the chicken is glazed and the internal temperature reaches 165°F.

VARIATION TIP: You can cook boneless, skinless chicken breasts or thighs with this method. Reduce the first cooking time to 13 minutes for breasts and 15 minutes for thighs.

# Orange Curried Chicken Stir-Fry

Serves **4 to 6** • DAIRY-FREE, GLUTEN-FREE

Setting: **Bake** • Temperature: **370°F** • Prep time: **12 minutes** • Cook time: **19 minutes**

*This easy stir-fry recipe is flavored with orange juice and curry powder, so it's sweet and spicy. For a quick dinner, serve over hot cooked rice with a green salad. Although there are many varieties of chutney, mango chutney is the most common and popular.*

1¼ pounds boneless, skinless chicken thighs, cut into 1-inch pieces

1 yellow bell pepper, cut into 1½-inch pieces

1 red bell pepper, cut into 1½-inch pieces

1 small red onion, sliced

⅓ cup chicken stock

⅓ cup orange juice

¼ cup mango chutney

2 tablespoons honey

2 tablespoons cornstarch

1 tablespoon curry powder

1. Preheat the air fryer by setting it to Bake and the temperature to 370°F.

2. Put the chicken thighs, yellow and red bell peppers, and onion on two racks in the air fryer. Bake for 12 to 14 minutes, or until the chicken is cooked to an internal temperature of 165°F. Remove the chicken and vegetables from the air fryer and set aside.

3. In an 8-inch metal bowl, stir together the stock, orange juice, chutney, honey, cornstarch, and curry powder. Stir in the chicken and vegetables and put the bowl into the air fryer.

4. Bake for 2 minutes. Remove the bowl from the air fryer and stir, then put it back into the air fryer and bake for 2 to 3 minutes more, or until the sauce is thickened and bubbly.

INGREDIENT TIP: Curry powder is not one single spice, but a combination of many spices. In India, many families have their own unique blend. There are many brands on the market; try a few to find your favorite.

# Chicken Fajitas

Serves **4 to 6** • GLUTEN-FREE

Setting: **Roast** • Temperature: **380°F** • Prep time: **12 minutes** • Cook time: **15 minutes**

*These fajitas are made with grilled chicken and vegetables, tossed with a spicy dressing and salsa, and served with lettuce and avocado in a soft corn tortilla. You can adjust the heat level according to your taste.*

5 boneless, skinless chicken breasts, cut into ½-inch-thick slices

2 red bell peppers, sliced

1 red onion, sliced

6 tablespoons spicy ranch salad dressing, divided

½ teaspoon dried oregano leaves

⅓ cup salsa

8 certified gluten-free corn tortillas

2 cups torn butter lettuce

2 avocados, peeled, pitted, and chopped

1. Preheat the air fryer by setting it to Roast and the temperature to 380°F.

2. Arrange the chicken on one rack and the bell peppers and onion on the other. Drizzle the chicken with 2 tablespoons of dressing and sprinkle with the oregano. Put the racks into the air fryer, with the chicken on the top rack.

3. Roast for 10 to 15 minutes, or until the internal temperature of the chicken reaches 165°F.

4. Transfer the chicken and vegetables to a serving bowl and toss with the remaining 4 tablespoons of dressing and the salsa.

5. Serve the chicken mixture with the tortillas, lettuce, and avocados.

VARIATION TIP: Use sliced boneless, skinless chicken thighs instead of chicken breasts. The cooking time will be a bit longer, 12 to 17 minutes.

# Tex-Mex Turkey Burgers

Serves **4** • GLUTEN-FREE

Setting: **Broil** • Temperature: **400°F** • Prep time: **12 minutes** • Cook time: **12 minutes**

*Turkey burgers are lower in fat than those made from ground beef. But they must still be cooked to well done, or 165°F, for food-safety reasons. In this recipe, bland turkey is made flavorful with crushed corn tortilla chips, pepper Jack cheese, and salsa.*

⅓ cup finely crushed certified gluten-free corn tortilla chips

1 large egg, beaten

⅓ cup salsa

½ cup shredded pepper Jack cheese

⅛ teaspoon kosher salt

Pinch cayenne pepper

1¼ pounds ground turkey

1 tablespoon olive oil

1 teaspoon paprika

1. In a medium bowl, combine the tortilla chips, egg, salsa, cheese, salt, and cayenne and mix well. Add the turkey and mix gently but thoroughly. Form the mixture into 4 patties about ½ inch thick. Make an indentation in the center of each patty with your thumb so the burgers do not puff up while cooking.

2. Brush the patties on both sides with oil and sprinkle with the paprika.

3. Line one of the air fryer racks with heavy-duty aluminum foil and place the burgers on the foil.

4. Preheat the air fryer by setting it to Broil and the temperature to 400°F.

5. Put the rack into the top area of the air fryer. Broil for 9 to 12 minutes, turning the burgers once halfway through the cooking time, until the internal temperature reaches 165°F.

VARIATION TIP: Serve these burgers in corn tortillas to continue the gluten-free theme, or serve them in toasted buns with avocados, more cheese, and more salsa. Or serve plain, topped with cheese and avocado.

# Bacon-Mustard Rotisserie Chicken

Serves **4 to 6** • DAIRY-FREE, GLUTEN-FREE

Setting: **Air Fry, Rotate** • Temperature: **400°F and 350°F** • Prep time: **17 minutes**

Cook time: **55 minutes to 1 hour 10 minutes**

*There's one trick to a rotisserie chicken: You must truss it so the wings and legs are held close to the body and don't overcook. Then the chicken will cook beautifully in the air fryer and the result is spectacular.*

3 bacon slices

¼ cup honey mustard

1 tablespoon apple juice

1 tablespoon lemon juice

1 (3- to 4-pound) whole
   chicken

1 thyme sprig

1. Preheat the air fryer by setting it to Air Fry and the temperature to 400°F.

2. Air fry the bacon for 8 to 10 minutes on one of the racks, or until crisp; or cook it on the stovetop. Remove the bacon and drain on paper towels. Reserve 1 tablespoon of bacon fat.

3. In a small bowl, whisk the honey mustard, apple juice, lemon juice, and reserved bacon fat to blend.

4. Remove and discard the chicken giblets from the chicken. Pat the chicken dry with paper towels.

5. Insert the bacon and thyme sprig into the chicken. Cut a piece of kitchen twine about 3 feet long. Place the chicken, breast-side up, on the twine. Wrap the twine around the chicken, pinning the wings to the body. Cross the twine under the chicken again and bring the twine down to the legs. Cross the legs, then tie the legs together firmly at the "ankles." Knot the twine and cut off the excess.

6. Rub the honey mustard mixture all over the chicken. Thread the rotisserie spit through the chicken, then fasten the forks firmly onto the chicken so it doesn't move.

7. Preheat the air fryer by setting it to Air Fry and the temperature to 350°F.

8. Add the drip pan to the fryer and use the rotisserie tool to place the chicken in the air fryer. If your air fryer does not have a rotisserie function, place the chicken on a rack or in the air fryer basket.

9. Press Start and Rotate and cook for 45 minutes. Check the internal temperature of the chicken in a couple of places; it should be 165°F. If not, cook for 5 to 15 minutes longer.

10. Remove the chicken from the air fryer, remove the chicken from the spit, cover, and let rest for 10 minutes before serving. (You can eat the bacon!)

INGREDIENT TIP: Make sure the chicken fits into your air fryer before you start this recipe. Most roasting chickens weigh 5 to 7 pounds, but a broiler-fryer is smaller, at 3 to 4 pounds. The broiler-fryer is the best size for the air fryer.

# Chicken Cordon Bleu

Serves **4**

Setting: **Air Fry** • Temperature: **380°F** • Prep time: **15 minutes** • Cook time: **15 minutes**

*"Cordon bleu" is French for "blue ribbon," and is the name of the famous cooking school in Paris. Chicken Cordon Bleu is chicken stuffed with ham and Swiss or Gruyere cheese, then rolled in breadcrumbs for a crispy crust. It's a fancy recipe that's a cinch to make in the air fryer.*

4 chicken breast fillets
⅓ cup chopped ham
½ cup shredded Swiss or
   Gruyere cheese
⅓ cup all-purpose flour
¼ teaspoon kosher salt
⅛ teaspoon freshly
   ground black pepper
1 teaspoon dried
   marjoram leaves
1 large egg
1½ cups panko
   breadcrumbs
Olive oil, for misting

1. Put the chicken breasts on a work surface and press gently with the palm of your hand to make them a bit thinner.

2. In a small bowl, combine the ham and cheese. Divide this mixture among the chicken. Wrap the chicken around the filling to enclose it, using toothpicks to hold the chicken together.

3. In a shallow bowl, whisk the flour, salt, pepper, and marjoram to blend. In another shallow bowl, beat the egg. Spread the breadcrumbs on a plate.

4. Dip the chicken into the flour mixture, shaking off any excess. Dip it into the egg, then into the breadcrumbs to coat, pressing the crumbs onto the chicken. At this point you can cover and refrigerate the chicken for up to 4 hours.

5. When you're ready to eat, preheat the air fryer by setting it to Air Fry and the temperature to 380°F.

6. Arrange the chicken on a rack and put the rack on the lowest level.

7. Air fry for 13 to 15 minutes, or until the internal temperature of the chicken reaches 165°F. Carefully remove the toothpicks and serve.

# Buttermilk Fried Chicken

Serves **4 to 6**

Setting: **Air Fry** • Temperature: **370°F** • Prep time: **10 minutes** • Cook time: **25 minutes**

*Buttermilk fried chicken is perhaps the most decadent of fried foods. But many people don't make it at home because oil spatters everywhere during cooking— and it's just not healthy to eat it too often. The air fryer comes to the rescue with this delicious adaptation so you can enjoy this tasty treat more often.*

8 chicken pieces (drumsticks, breasts, and thighs)

1 cup all-purpose flour

2 teaspoons paprika

½ teaspoon kosher salt

Freshly ground black pepper

½ cup buttermilk

2 large eggs

2 tablespoons olive oil

1½ cups soft, fresh breadcrumbs

**VARIATION TIP:**
Marinate the chicken in buttermilk and spices such as cayenne pepper, garlic powder, or chili powder in the refrigerator overnight before you cook it. This makes the chicken even more moist and tender and adds great flavor.

1. Pat the chicken dry. Do not rinse the chicken for food-safety reasons.

2. In a shallow bowl, whisk the flour, paprika, salt, and pepper to taste to blend.

3. In another shallow bowl, beat the buttermilk with the eggs until combined.

4. In a third shallow bowl, stir together the oil and breadcrumbs until mixed.

5. Dredge the chicken in the flour to coat, shake off any excess, then dip the chicken into the eggs to coat. Finally, dip the chicken into the breadcrumbs, patting the crumbs firmly onto the skin.

6. Preheat the air fryer by setting it to Air Fry and the temperature to 370°F.

7. Arrange the chicken in a single layer on both racks.

8. Air fry the chicken for 20 to 25 minutes, or until the internal temperature of the chicken reaches 165°F and the chicken is brown and crisp. Let cool for 5 minutes, then serve.

# Ham and Cheese–Stuffed Chicken Burgers

**Serves 4**

Setting: **Air Fry** • Temperature: **350°F** • Prep time: **12 minutes** • Cook time: **16 minutes**

*This fun take on a chicken burger is more interesting and complex, but still easy to make. The ham and cheese are delicious against the mild chicken. Serve these flavorful, juicy burgers on toasted onion buns slathered with mayo and mustard and piled high with sliced tomatoes.*

½ cup soft, fresh breadcrumbs

3 tablespoons whole milk

1 large egg, beaten

1 teaspoon dried thyme leaves

¼ teaspoon kosher salt

1¼ pounds ground chicken

⅓ cup finely chopped ham

½ cup shredded Havarti or Swiss cheese

Olive oil, for misting

1. In a medium bowl, combine the breadcrumbs, milk, egg, thyme, and salt and mix well. Add the ground chicken and mix gently but thoroughly.

2. Form the chicken into 8 thin patties and place on wax paper. Top 4 patties with ham and cheese, leaving a 1-inch border. Top with the remaining 4 patties and press the edges together gently to seal and enclose the ham and cheese.

3. Preheat the air fryer by setting it to Air Fry and the temperature to 350°F.

4. Place the burgers on parchment paper on one of the oven racks and place the rack on the lower level. Mist with oil.

5. Air fry for 13 to 16 minutes, or until the internal temperature of the chicken reaches 165°F. Make sure the thermometer does not reach the filling in the center of the burger for accurate results.

INGREDIENT TIP: You can buy chopped ham for this recipe or buy a slice of ham and chop it yourself. The pieces should be no larger than ½ inch square.

# Chicken Tenders with Veggies

Serves **4 to 6** • DAIRY-FREE

Setting: **Air Fry** • Temperature: **380°F** • Prep time: **12 minutes** • Cook time: **20 minutes**

*Chicken tenders are actually part of the breast; they are tender and easy to cook and beloved by children. In this recipe, the tenders are coated with honey and seasoned breadcrumbs and they cook up crisp and juicy.*

1½ pounds chicken tenders

2 tablespoons honey

½ teaspoon kosher salt

1½ cups soft, fresh breadcrumbs

1 teaspoon dried thyme leaves

2 tablespoons olive oil, divided

2 carrots, sliced

15 creamer potatoes or tiny red potatoes, halved

1. In a medium bowl, toss the chicken tenders with the honey and salt to coat.

2. In a shallow bowl, stir together the breadcrumbs, thyme, and 1 tablespoon of oil.

3. Coat the tenders in the breadcrumbs, pressing them firmly onto the meat. Arrange the tenders on one of the air fryer racks.

4. Place the carrots and potatoes on the second air fryer rack and drizzle with the remaining 1 tablespoon of oil.

5. Preheat the air fryer by setting it to Air Fry and the temperature to 380°F.

6. Put the rack with the chicken in the top slot, and the rack with the vegetables in a lower slot.

7. Air fry for 18 to 20 minutes, or until the internal temperature of the chicken reaches 165°F and the vegetables are tender.

VARIATION TIP: For a spicier recipe, coat the chicken tenders in a combination of Sriracha and honey. Or use adobo sauce from a jar of chipotle peppers in adobo, or just add ⅛ teaspoon cayenne pepper to the honey mixture.

*Meatballs in Spicy Tomato Sauce, page 96*

✦

# BEEF, PORK, AND LAMB

# Rotisserie Pork Tenderloin

Serves **4 to 6** • DAIRY-FREE

Setting: **Air Fry, Rotate** • Temperature: **350°F**

Prep time: **20 minutes, plus 6 hours to marinate** • Cook time: **30 minutes**

*Pork tenderloin cooks beautifully on the rotisserie. There's just one trick: Use two tenderloins and tie them together around the spit so they cook evenly.*

2 (1-pound) pork tenderloins

⅓ cup prune juice

⅓ cup ketchup

¼ cup packed brown sugar

3 tablespoons low-sodium soy sauce

1 pound creamer potatoes or tiny red potatoes, halved

8 ounces baby carrots, halved lengthwise

1 tablespoon olive oil

INGREDIENT TIP: Don't be turned off by the prune juice; it makes the pork so tender and adds an irresistible, rich flavor.

1. Prick the pork all over with a fork. In a large, shallow bowl, stir together the prune juice, ketchup, brown sugar, and soy sauce. Add the pork and turn to coat. Cover and refrigerate for 3 to 6 hours, or up to 24 hours.

2. Drain off the marinade and discard. Place the tenderloins on the rotisserie spit, one on each side, pairing the wide end of one tenderloin with the thin end of the other to make an even bundle. Tie firmly with kitchen twine at 3-inch intervals. Firmly attach the rotisserie forks to the pork.

3. Place the potatoes and carrots on a rimmed sheet pan and drizzle with the oil.

4. Preheat the air fryer by setting it to Air Fry and the temperature to 350°F.

5. Put the potatoes and carrots in the bottom of the air fryer and attach the rotisserie using the rotisserie tool. If your air fryer does not have a rotisserie function, arrange the tenderloins on a rack or in the air fryer basket (the cooking time will be cut in half).

6. Press Start and Rotate. Cook for 25 to 30 minutes, or until the internal temperature of the pork reaches at least 145°F and the vegetables are tender.

# Thai-Flavored Burgers

Serves **4** • DAIRY-FREE

Setting: **Broil** • Temperature: **380°F** • Prep time: **12 minutes** • Cook time: **15 minutes**

*Did you know that ground beef must be cooked to 160°F for food-safety reasons? This can make burgers dry and tough, but adding a mixture of crumbs and liquid to the meat lets you cook that burger to a safe temperature and still be moist and delicious.*

½ cup soft, fresh
   breadcrumbs
¼ cup Thai chili sauce
2 scallions, green parts
   only, minced
2 garlic cloves, minced
1¼ pounds 93 percent
   lean ground beef
4 onion rolls, split
1 large beefsteak tomato,
   sliced
⅓ cup peanut sauce

1. In a large bowl, combine the breadcrumbs, chili sauce, scallions, and garlic and mix. Add the beef and mix gently but thoroughly. Form the beef mixture into 4 patties. Make an indentation into the center of each patty so the burgers don't puff up when they cook.

2. Preheat the air fryer by setting it to Broil and the temperature to 380°F.

3. Line an air fryer rack with aluminum foil and place the burgers on the foil. Insert the rack into the top slots in the air fryer.

4. Cook for 12 minutes, flipping once during cooking, and then test the burgers. If they aren't at least 160°F, cook for 2 to 3 minutes more.

5. Assemble the burgers on the onion rolls and top with tomato and peanut sauce to serve.

VARIATION TIP: Make these burgers with ground pork or a combination of ground pork and ground beef. Just make sure the burgers are cooked to 160°F.

# Beef Korma

Serves **4 to 6** • GLUTEN-FREE

Setting: **Air Fry** • Temperature: **350°F** • Prep time: **15 minutes** • Cook time: **20 minutes**

*Beef korma is an Indian recipe made of a mixture of meat and vegetables cooked in a yogurt sauce seasoned generously with curry powder. This recipe can be mild or spicy, depending on your taste and the spiciness of the curry powder you use. Serve over hot cooked rice, if desired.*

1¼ pounds sirloin steak, cut against the grain into ½-inch-thick slices

½ cup plain yogurt

1 to 2 tablespoons curry powder

2 teaspoons olive oil

1 onion, chopped

2 garlic cloves, minced

2 beefsteak tomatoes, diced

1 cup frozen baby peas, thawed

1. Preheat the air fryer by setting it to Air Fry and the temperature to 350°F.

2. In a medium bowl, stir together the steak, yogurt, and curry powder. Set aside for 10 minutes.

3. In an 8-inch metal bowl, stir together the oil, onion, and garlic. Place the bowl in the air fryer and cook for 3 to 4 minutes, or until the onion and garlic are tender.

4. Add the steak mixture to the bowl, along with the tomatoes. Air fry for 12 to 13 minutes, or until the steak is almost tender.

5. Stir in the peas and cook for 2 to 3 minutes, or until hot.

INGREDIENT TIP: The best beef cuts for this recipe include sirloin, sirloin tip, and top round. The yogurt makes the steak tender, even with the short marinating time.

# Rice and Meatball–Stuffed Peppers

Serves **4** • DAIRY-FREE, GLUTEN-FREE

Setting: **Bake** • Temperature: **400°F** • Prep time: **14 minutes** • Cook time: **20 minutes**

*Stuffed peppers are classic comfort food. The peppers are usually stuffed with a variety of vegetables along with rice and cheese; meatballs make this dish heartier. You can choose any color of bell pepper you want—mix and match if you like! Choose the tiny appetizer-size meatballs for this delicious dish.*

4 large bell peppers

1 tablespoon olive oil

1 onion, chopped

3 garlic cloves, minced

1½ cups frozen cooked rice, thawed

20 small frozen precooked meatballs, thawed

½ cup tomato sauce

2 tablespoons Dijon mustard

1. Preheat the air fryer by setting it to Bake and the temperature to 400°F.

2. Cut off about ½ inch of the pepper tops (save for another use). Carefully remove the membranes and seeds from the peppers. Set the peppers aside.

3. In a 7-inch round baking pan, stir together the oil, onion, and garlic. Bake for 2 to 4 minutes, or until crisp-tender. Transfer the vegetables from the pan to a medium bowl.

4. Stir the rice, meatballs, tomato sauce, and mustard into the vegetable mixture and stuff the filling into the peppers.

5. Place the peppers on an air fryer rack and insert the rack into the lowest level of the air fryer. Bake for 13 to 16 minutes, or until the filling is hot and the peppers are tender.

INGREDIENT TIP: Make sure that the meatballs, tomato sauce, and mustard you buy are gluten-free for this recipe if you cannot eat wheat or gluten. And if you can't find small meatballs, cut regular-size meatballs into halves or quarters so they fit easily into the peppers.

# Unstuffed Cabbage

Serves **4 to 6** • DAIRY-FREE, GLUTEN-FREE

Setting: **Bake** • Temperature: **370°F** • Prep time: **10 minutes** • Cook time: **21 minutes**

*Making traditional stuffed cabbage is a bit of work. You have to soften the cabbage leaves, make the filling, stuff the leaves, then roll them up, and bake the dish. This unstuffed version tastes like the real thing, but with much less work.*

1 tablespoon olive oil

1 onion, chopped

2 cups chopped green
   cabbage

16 precooked frozen
   meatballs

1½ cups frozen cooked
   rice

2 tomatoes, chopped

1 teaspoon dried
   marjoram leaves

¼ teaspoon kosher salt

Freshly ground black
   pepper

1. Preheat the air fryer by setting it to Bake and the temperature to 370°F.

2. In an 8-inch metal bowl, stir together the oil and onion. Bake for 2 to 4 minutes, or until the onion is tender.

3. Add the cabbage, meatballs, rice, tomatoes, marjoram, salt, and pepper to taste to the bowl and stir.

4. Bake for 12 to 17 minutes, stirring once during cooking time, until the mixture is hot, the vegetables are tender, and the internal temperature of the meatballs reaches 160°F.

INGREDIENT TIP: You can buy prepared fresh veggies at most supermarkets, including chopped onion and chopped cabbage for slaw, which will significantly reduce the preparation time for this recipe.

# Honey Mustard Lamb Chops

Serves **4**  •  DAIRY-FREE, GLUTEN-FREE

Setting: **Air Fry**  •  Temperature: **390°F**

Prep time: **10 minutes, plus 15 minutes to marinate**  •  Cook time: **12 minutes**

*Lamb is a very rich meat; the fat really coats your tongue as you eat it. That's why lamb is usually served with a strongly flavored sauce like currant jelly or mint; it cuts through the fat and balances the dish. In this recipe, mustard adds a spicy note to tender chops.*

2 tablespoons apple cider vinegar

1 tablespoon olive oil

1 teaspoon dried oregano leaves

1½ pounds bone-in lamb loin chops

3 tablespoons honey mustard

½ teaspoon garlic powder

¼ teaspoon kosher salt

1. In a shallow bowl, combine the vinegar, oil, and oregano. Add the lamb chops and turn to coat. Let stand for 15 minutes.

2. Preheat the air fryer by setting it to Air Fry and the temperature to 390°F.

3. In another shallow bowl, stir together the honey mustard, garlic powder, and salt. Remove the lamb chops from the marinade and coat them in the mustard mixture. Arrange the chops on the air fryer racks in a single layer.

4. Air fry for 8 to 12 minutes, or until the internal temperature of the chops reaches at least 145°F.

INGREDIENT TIP: Loin chops have a T-bone–shaped bone in the center; this is different from rack of lamb chops, which have a bone extending from the meat. Both work well in this recipe, but you can fit more loin chops on an air fryer rack.

# Meatballs in Spicy Tomato Sauce

Serves **4 to 6** • DAIRY-FREE

Setting: **Bake** • Temperature: **400°F** • Prep time: **15 minutes** • Cook time: **16 minutes**

*These meatballs may become your air fryer go-to. You can make moist meat-balls with a slightly crisp crust with much less effort than making them on the stovetop. Dijon mustard adds a spicy note to the pasta sauce. Serve over hot cooked pasta, mashed potatoes, or rice.*

⅓ cup crushed saltine
  cracker crumbs
3 scallions, green parts
  only, minced
1 large egg
2 garlic cloves, minced
¼ teaspoon kosher salt
Freshly ground black
  pepper
1⅓ pounds 95 percent
  lean ground beef
1½ cups jarred marinara
  sauce
2 tablespoons Dijon
  mustard

1. In a large bowl, combine the cracker crumbs, scallions, egg, garlic, salt, and pepper to taste and mix. Add the ground beef and mix gently. Form the meat mixture into 1½-inch meatballs.

2. Preheat the air fryer by setting it to Bake and the temperature to 400°F.

3. Arrange the meatballs on the two air fryer racks. Bake for 8 to 12 minutes, or until the internal temperature of the meatballs reaches 160°F.

4. Remove the meatballs from the air fryer and place them in an 8-inch metal bowl. Add the marinara and mustard and mix gently. Bake for 3 to 4 minutes, or until the sauce is hot.

# Mexican Pizza

Serves **4 to 6**

Setting: **Bake** • Temperature: **370°F** • Prep time: **12 minutes** • Cook time: **10 minutes**

*Pizza cooks quickly—and beautifully—in the air fryer! The crust gets crispy and the cheese melts to perfection. This recipe is a spicy twist on classic pizza. The refried beans add a rich note and the salsa and jalapeño pepper add a nice kick.*

1 cup canned refried
    beans
1 cup salsa
6 fully cooked pork
    breakfast sausages,
    chopped
1 jalapeño pepper, diced
6 whole wheat pita breads
1 cup shredded pepper
    Jack cheese
1 cup shredded Colby or
    Cheddar cheese
½ cup sour cream
1 avocado, peeled, pitted,
    and diced

1. Preheat the air fryer by setting it to Bake and the temperature to 370°F.

2. In a medium bowl, stir together the refried beans, salsa, sausage, and jalapeño. Spoon and spread this mixture onto the pita breads and sprinkle with the pepper Jack and Colby cheeses.

3. Arrange the pizza on the two air fryer racks. Bake for 7 to 10 minutes, or until the pizzas are crisp and the cheese melts and starts to brown.

4. Top each pizza with a dollop of sour cream and some avocado and serve hot.

VARIATION TIP: Use other meats on this pizza. Add cooked crumbled sausage or ground beef, or add more vegetables, like bell pepper, red onion, or chopped tomato.

# Tex-Mex Steak

Serves **4 to 6** • DAIRY-FREE, GLUTEN-FREE

Setting: **Broil** • Temperature: **390°F** • Prep time: **25 minutes, plus 20 minutes to marinate**

Cook time: **10 minutes, plus 10 minutes to rest**

*Who needs a grill when you have an air fryer? Most of the prep time in this recipe is marinating time, so you can prepare other components of the meal, such as a salad, while you wait. The classic spicy flavors of Mexican dishes come from chipotle peppers and red pepper flakes.*

1½ pounds skirt steak
2 chipotle peppers in adobo sauce, minced (La Costeña or another gluten-free brand)
½ teaspoon kosher salt
¼ teaspoon freshly ground black pepper
¼ teaspoon red pepper flakes

1. Cut the steak into 6 pieces and place them on a plate.

2. In a small bowl, stir together the chipotle peppers and adobo sauce, salt, black pepper, and red pepper flakes. Spread the chiles over the steaks on both sides. Let the steaks stand at room temperature for at least 20 minutes, or up to 1 hour, or cover and refrigerate for up to 12 hours.

3. Preheat the air fryer by setting it to Broil and the temperature to 390°F.

4. Arrange the steaks on an air fryer rack and place the rack in the upper slots in the appliance. Broil for 10 minutes, turning once, until the internal temperature of the steaks reaches at least 145°F.

5. Remove the steaks, cover, and let rest for 10 minutes. Thinly slice the steaks across the grain to serve.

INGREDIENT TIP: Chipotles in adobo are smoked jalapeño peppers that are jarred in a spicy red sauce. They are spicy and sweet and smoky tasting. Many brands contain gluten, so read the label carefully if you are gluten-free.

# Tender Country Ribs

Serves **4 to 6** • DAIRY-FREE, GLUTEN-FREE

Setting: **Roast** • Temperature: **400°F** • Prep time: **5 minutes** • Cook time: **25 minutes**

*Country-style pork ribs are much meatier than spareribs. You can buy them with or without the bone, but for this recipe, opt for boneless ribs. When ribs are cooked in the air fryer, you get the depth of flavor of traditional ribs in a fraction of the time.*

16 boneless country-style pork ribs, trimmed of **excess fat**

3 tablespoons cornstarch

3 tablespoons olive oil

1 teaspoon ground mustard

1 teaspoon dried thyme leaves

1 teaspoon dried marjoram leaves

½ teaspoon garlic powder

¼ teaspoon kosher salt

Freshly ground black pepper

1. Place the ribs on a clean work surface.

2. In a small bowl, stir together the cornstarch, oil, ground mustard, thyme, marjoram, garlic powder, salt, and pepper to taste. Rub the marinade into the ribs.

3. Preheat the air fryer by setting it to Roast and the temperature to 400°F.

4. Place the ribs on the air fryer racks and insert the racks into the air fryer. Roast for 10 minutes. Turn the ribs with tongs and roast for 10 to 15 minutes more, or until the ribs are crisp and the internal temperature reaches at least 150°F.

INGREDIENT TIP: When you turn the ribs, you may want to remove excess grease from the drip pan to prevent smoking. Carefully discard the fat, which you can freeze and put into the garbage. Never pour hot fat down the kitchen drain!

# Bacon-Garlic Pizza

Serves **4 to 6**

Setting: **Bake** • Temperature: **370°F** • Prep time: **15 minutes**

Cook time: **12 minutes per batch**

*Frozen dinner rolls make great crusts for individual pizzas. The dough is firmer than most pizza dough and makes a crispier crust. The Dijon mustard adds the perfect amount of spiciness to the sauce. These individual pizzas are fun to make and eat.*

All-purpose flour, for dusting

Nonstick baking spray

6 frozen large whole wheat dinner rolls, thawed

1 cup pizza sauce

2 tablespoons Dijon mustard

6 garlic cloves, minced

1 teaspoon dried oregano leaves

½ teaspoon garlic salt

10 precooked bacon slices, cut into 1-inch pieces

1¾ cups shredded Cheddar cheese

1. Lightly dust a work surface with flour and put the rolls on it. Press each dinner roll into a 6 × 3-inch oval.

2. Line the air fryer racks with parchment paper and coat the paper with baking spray. Place 3 flattened rolls on each rack with about ½ inch of space between them.

3. Preheat the air fryer by setting it to Bake and the temperature to 370°F.

4. Insert the racks in the fryer and bake the flattened rolls for 2 minutes, or until they are set but not brown.

5. Meanwhile, in a small bowl, stir together the pizza sauce, mustard, garlic, oregano, and garlic salt. When the crusts are set, spread each with some of the sauce. Top with the bacon pieces and cheese.

6. Bake for 8 to 10 minutes, or until the crusts are brown and the cheese is melted and starting to brown. If you are using a smaller air fryer, you may need to cook the pizzas in batches. In that case, add the sauce and toppings to the crusts just before baking.

*Marble Cheesecake, page* 107

# CHAPTER NINE

◆

# DESSERTS AND BAKED TREATS

# Broiled Curried Fruit

Serves **4 to 6** • DAIRY-FREE, GLUTEN-FREE

Setting: **Broil** • Temperature: **350°F** • Prep time: **10 minutes** • Cook time: **7 minutes**

*If you have never had broiled fruit, this recipe is a wonderful introduction. Broiling caramelizes the sugars in the fruit, brings out their flavor, and even turns fruit that's not quite ripe in a sweet and quick dessert. Serve over ice cream or sherbet, if you like.*

2 peaches

2 firm pears

3 plums

1 tablespoon lemon juice

2 tablespoons butter, melted

1 tablespoon honey

2 tablespoons brown sugar

2 to 3 teaspoons curry powder

1. Halve the peaches and remove their pits. Halve the pears, core them, then remove the stem. Halve the plums and remove their pits.

2. Arrange the fruits, cut-side up, on one of the air fryer racks. Drizzle the fruit with the lemon juice, butter, and honey and sprinkle with the brown sugar and curry powder.

3. Preheat the air fryer by setting it to Broil and the temperature to 350°F.

4. Broil the fruits on the top rack for 3 to 7 minutes, or until the fruits are soft and tender.

INGREDIENT TIP: The lemon juice contains ascorbic acid, which prevents enzymatic browning when fruits such as apples and pears are cut. It also adds a bit of bright flavor.

# Orange Cornmeal Cake

Serves **4 to 6** • DAIRY-FREE, VEGETARIAN

Setting: **Bake** • Temperature: **340°F** • Prep time: **10 minutes** • Cook time: **23 minutes**

*Cornmeal adds wonderful flavor and a bit of crunch to this tender cake recipe. An orange glaze is poured over the cake while it's still hot and soaks into the crumb. Serve this cake with a cup of coffee for breakfast or an afternoon snack.*

Nonstick cooking spray
1¼ cups all-purpose flour
¾ cup granulated sugar
½ cup yellow cornmeal
1 teaspoon baking soda
¼ cup safflower oil
1¼ cups orange juice, divided
1 teaspoon vanilla extract
¼ cup powdered sugar

1. Preheat the air fryer by setting it to Bake and the temperature to 340°F. Coat a 6-inch round baking pan with cooking spray and set aside.

2. In a medium bowl, whisk the flour, granulated sugar, cornmeal, baking soda, oil, 1 cup of orange juice, and the vanilla until smooth. Pour the batter into the prepared pan and place it in the air fryer.

3. Bake for 20 to 23 minutes, or until a toothpick inserted into the center of the cake comes out clean. The cake will also be pulling away from the sides of the pan.

4. Remove the cake from the air fryer and place on a cooling rack. Using a toothpick, make about 20 holes in the cake.

5. In a small bowl, whisk the remaining ¼ cup of orange juice and powdered sugar until smooth and well mixed. Slowly drizzle the glaze over the hot cake.

6. Cool completely, then carefully remove the cake from the pan and cut into wedges to serve.

VARIATION TIP: Make this a lemon cake: Substitute freshly squeezed lemon juice for the orange juice.

# Black Forest Hand Pies

Makes **9 hand pies** • VEGETARIAN

Setting: **Bake** • Temperature: **300°F** • Prep time: **12 minutes**

Cook time: **13 minutes, plus 20 minutes to cool**

*Hand pies are little pies that you can, well, hold in your hand! Black Forest torte is an Old-World cake recipe that combines chocolate and cherries. This recipe is a mashup of both, encased in puff pastry that cooks to perfection in the air fryer. You can serve these hand pies warm or cold.*

3 tablespoons milk chocolate or dark chocolate chips

2 tablespoons thick hot fudge sauce

2 tablespoons chopped dried cherries

All-purpose flour, for dusting

1 (10 × 11-inch) sheet puff pastry, thawed

1 large egg, beaten

2 tablespoons sugar

½ teaspoon ground cinnamon

INGREDIENT TIP:
Puff pastry is usually thawed in the fridge overnight, but you can also thaw it on the counter in about 20 minutes. Don't let it get too warm though, or the pastry will not puff as it bakes.

1. In a small bowl, stir together the chocolate chips, fudge sauce, and cherries.

2. Dust a work surface with flour and put the puff pastry on it. Roll the puff pastry into a 12-inch square. Using a sharp knife, cut the pastry into 9 squares.

3. Place about 2 teaspoons of the chocolate mixture into the center of each square. Brush the edges with the beaten egg. Fold the squares in half to make triangles. Firmly press the edges with a fork to seal.

4. Very lightly brush the triangles on all sides with more of the beaten egg and sprinkle with sugar and cinnamon.

5. Preheat the air fryer by setting it to Bake and the temperature to 300°F.

6. Arrange the triangles on the air fryer racks, leaving about 1 inch of space between each. Bake for 10 to 13 minutes, or until golden brown and crisp. Cool on a wire rack for at least 20 minutes before serving.

# Marble Cheesecake

Serves **4 to 6** • VEGETARIAN

Setting: **Bake** • Temperature: **320°F**

Prep time: **12 minutes, plus 10 minutes to freeze and 3 hours to chill**

Cook time: **20 minutes**

*A cheesecake cooked in the air fryer seems improbable, but it works! This delicious concoction combines vanilla and chocolate for a gorgeous dessert.*

1 cup graham cracker crumbs

3 tablespoons butter, at room temperature

1½ (8-ounce) packages cream cheese, at room temperature

⅓ cup sugar

2 large eggs, beaten

1 tablespoon all-purpose flour

1 teaspoon vanilla extract

¼ cup chocolate syrup

1. Preheat the air fryer by setting it to Bake and the temperature to 320°F.

2. In a small bowl, stir together the graham cracker crumbs and butter thoroughly. Press the crumbs into the bottom of a 6-inch round baking pan and freeze for about 10 minutes, or until the filling is ready.

3. Meanwhile, in a medium bowl, mix the cream cheese and sugar well. One at a time, beat in the eggs. Add the flour and vanilla and mix well.

4. Transfer ⅔ cup of filling to a small bowl and stir in the chocolate syrup until combined.

5. Pour the vanilla filling over the crust. Drop the chocolate filling on top by the spoonful. With a clean butter knife or small spatula, combine the fillings in a zigzag pattern to marble. Be careful not to disturb the crust on the bottom of the pan.

6. Bake for 20 minutes, or until the cheesecake is just set. Transfer the cheesecake to a wire rack and carefully run a knife around the edges to loosen the cheesecake from the sides of the pan. Cool for 1 hour, cover, and refrigerate for 2 to 3 hours longer, or until cold. Cut into wedges to serve.

# Black and White Brownies

Serves **6** • VEGETARIAN

Setting: **Bake** • Temperature: **340°F** • Prep time: **12 minutes**

Cook time: **20 minutes, plus 30 minutes to cool**

*Who doesn't love brownies? In the air fryer, the brownies stay moist and deeply rich, but they develop a wonderfully crunchy and crispy top. This easy recipe should quickly become part of your repertoire. Vary it as you like by adding different types of chips or frost it with a simple frosting, either from a can or homemade.*

1 large egg

¼ cup packed brown sugar

2 tablespoons granulated sugar

2 tablespoons safflower oil

1 teaspoon vanilla extract

⅓ cup all-purpose flour

¼ cup cocoa powder

¼ cup white chocolate chips

Nonstick cooking spray

1. Preheat the air fryer by setting it to Bake and the temperature to 340°F.

2. In a medium bowl, beat the egg, brown sugar, and granulated sugar until smooth. Beat in the oil and vanilla.

3. Add the flour and cocoa powder and mix just until combined. Fold in the chocolate chips.

4. Coat a 6-inch baking pan with cooking spray. Spoon the brownie mixture into the prepared pan and smooth the top.

5. Bake for 15 to 20 minutes, or until the brownies are set when lightly touched with your finger and the crust is shiny. Let cool on a wire rack for at least 30 minutes before slicing to serve.

INGREDIENT TIP: Cocoa powder is measured just like flour, by spooning it lightly into the measuring cup and leveling off with the back of a knife. Never scoop flour or dry ingredients directly using the cup because you will add too much and your cookies, cakes, and bars will be dense and heavy.

# Deconstructed Apple Crisp

Serves **4** • VEGETARIAN

Setting: **Air Fry, Rotate** • Temperature: **350°F** • Prep time: **15 minutes**

Cook time: **11 minutes**

*If you feel that apple crisp never has enough streusel, this is the recipe for you. Apples are roasted on the rotisserie while oatmeal streusel bakes underneath. Then the apples are topped with salted caramel sauce and the streusel.*

2 Granny Smith apples, peeled, halved, and cored

2 tablespoons lemon juice

2 tablespoons granulated sugar

½ teaspoon ground cinnamon

⅓ cup quick cooking oatmeal

⅓ cup all-purpose flour

¼ cup packed brown sugar

3 tablespoons butter, melted

¼ cup salted caramel sauce

1. Drizzle the apples with lemon juice. In a small bowl, stir together the granulated sugar and cinnamon and sprinkle over the apples. Put the apple halves back together and thread onto the rotisserie spit. Insert the spit forks, securing the apples.

2. Preheat the air fryer by setting it to Air Fry and the temperature to 350°F.

3. In a small bowl, stir together the oatmeal, flour, and brown sugar. Stir in the butter until crumbly. Put the mixture into the drip pan. Place the drip pan in the bottom of the air fryer. Carefully put the apples into the air fryer using the rotisserie tool.

4. Set the time for 10 minutes, then press Start and Rotate. If your air fryer does not have a rotisserie, arrange the apples on a rack and the streusel on a baking sheet on another rack.

5. At 8 minutes, pierce the apples with a fork. If not tender, cook for 2 to 3 minutes more.

6. When the streusel is light golden brown, remove from the air fryer. Place the apples on plates, cut-side up, spoon 1 tablespoon of caramel sauce over each, and sprinkle with streusel.

# Lemon Cranberry Bread Pudding

Serves **4 to 6** • VEGETARIAN

Setting: **Bake** • Temperature: **330°F** • Prep time: **20 minutes** • Cook time: **14 minutes**

*Bread pudding is the ultimate comfort food. The combination of lemon curd and dried cranberries adds brightness. Serve with whipped cream mixed with more lemon curd for a cool and flavorful topping.*

Nonstick cooking spray

2 large eggs

½ cup whole milk

½ cup lemon curd, divided

3 tablespoons freshy squeezed lemon juice

½ teaspoon grated lemon zest

⅓ cup sugar

1 teaspoon vanilla extract

6 slices firm white bread, cubed

½ cup dried cranberries

½ cup heavy (whipping) cream

1 tablespoon crushed hard lemon candy

1. Coat a 7-inch metal baking pan with cooking spray.

2. In a large bowl, whisk the eggs, milk, ¼ cup of lemon curd, lemon juice, lemon zest, sugar, and vanilla until combined. Stir in the bread cubes and cranberries and let soak for 10 minutes.

3. Preheat the air fryer by setting it to Bake and the temperature to 330°F.

4. Spoon the bread pudding into the prepared pan. Bake for 10 to 14 minutes, or until the pudding is firm to the touch.

5. In a large bowl, using a hand mixer on high speed, beat the cream for 3 to 4 minutes until stiff peaks form and fold in the remaining ¼ cup of lemon curd. Top the pudding with the whipped cream and garnish with the crushed lemon candy.

INGREDIENT TIP: There are many varieties of lemon curd on the market. Have a taste test to see which brand you prefer. They are all tart and sweet and are excellent additions to your pantry.

# Strawberry-Lime Fruit Leather

Serves **4 to 6** • DAIRY-FREE, GLUTEN-FREE, VEGAN

Setting: **Dehydrate** • Temperature: **135°F** • Prep time: **12 minutes**

Cook time: **12 hours**

*Fruit leather is a great sweet snack that kids love. The banana in this recipe adds a touch of sweetness and helps the leather hold together and gives it structure. The addition of strawberries and lime juice and zest is delicious. You'll need a five-layer round dehydrator rack for this recipe. You can also buy special fruit leather trays.*

8 cups hulled fresh
   strawberries

1 ripe banana

Grated zest of 1 lime

Juice of 1 lime

1. Preheat the air fryer by setting it to Dehydrate and the temperature to 135°F.

2. In a blender or food processor, blend or process the strawberries, banana, lime zest, and lime juice until smooth. Strain this mixture through a fine-mesh sieve to remove the strawberry seeds.

3. Line the dehydrator trays with silicone mats. Spread the strawberry mixture evenly on the mats to within about 1 inch from the edges. If you are using fruit leather trays, fill them evenly. The mixture should be about ¼ inch thick.

4. Dehydrate for 8 to 12 hours, or until the leather peels easily away from the mat or trays.

5. Cut the fruit leather into strips and lay them onto strips of parchment paper. Roll up the paper and tie with kitchen twine to store.

VARIATION TIP: Use other fruits in place of the strawberries. Try raspberries or even drained canned pineapple. You'll need about 4 cups of pureed fruit to make this recipe.

# Cinnamon Monkey Bread

Serves **4 to 6** • VEGETARIAN

Setting: **Bake** • Temperature: **350°F** • Prep time: **10 minutes** • Cook time: **9 minutes**

*Monkey bread is a sweet bread that can be served for dessert or breakfast. It's a strange name for a breakfast pastry, but it's delicious! Biscuit dough is cut into small pieces and coated in butter, sugar, and spices, then piled into a pan and baked. When it's done baking, the bread is frosted, then cooled for a bit, then everyone pulls off pieces to enjoy.*

Nonstick baking spray

1 (8-ounce) can refrigerated biscuits

¼ cup granulated sugar

3 tablespoons brown sugar

½ teaspoon ground cinnamon

⅛ teaspoon ground nutmeg

4 tablespoons (½ stick) unsalted butter, melted and divided

⅓ cup powdered sugar

1. Preheat the air fryer by setting it to Bake and the temperature to 350°F. Coat a 6-inch round baking pan with baking spray.

2. Separate the biscuits and cut each biscuit into 4 pieces.

3. In a shallow bowl, stir together the granulated sugar, brown sugar, cinnamon, and nutmeg. Place 3 tablespoons of melted butter in another shallow bowl.

4. Dip each biscuit piece briefly into the butter, then roll it in the sugar mixture to coat. Arrange the pieces in the prepared pan in an even layer.

5. Bake for 6 to 9 minutes, or until the bread is golden brown.

6. Meanwhile, in a small bowl, combine the powdered sugar with the remaining 1 tablespoon of melted butter and whisk until smooth.

7. When the bread is done, let cool for 5 minutes, then drizzle with the icing and serve. Be careful eating this bread at first, because the sugar gets very hot.

# Chocolate Peanut Butter Molten Cupcakes

Makes **8 cupcakes** • VEGETARIAN

Setting: **Bake** • Temperature: **320°F** • Prep time: **10 minutes** • Cook time: **13 minutes**

*Molten cupcakes are slightly underbaked so the center is soft and liquid when served. This recipe is a bit different. A ball of peanut butter and powdered sugar is placed in the middle of each cupcake, softening as the cupcake bakes, creating a molten middle of sweet peanut butter. Serve these cupcakes warm with vanilla or chocolate ice cream.*

1⅓ cups chocolate cake mix (from a 15-ounce box)

½ cup sour cream

¼ cup safflower oil

¼ cup hot water

1 large egg

1 large egg yolk

3 tablespoons peanut butter

1 tablespoon powdered sugar

INGREDIENT TIP: Save the rest of the cake mix in a zip-top bag and store at room temperature to make more cupcakes. Be sure to write the expiration date of the cake mix on the bag.

1. Preheat the air fryer by setting it to Bake and the temperature to 320°F. Double up 16 foil muffin cups to make 8 cups.

2. In a medium bowl, combine the cake mix, sour cream, oil, hot water, egg, and egg yolk. Beat until combined.

3. In a small bowl, stir together the peanut butter and powdered sugar until smooth. Form this mixture into 8 balls.

4. Spoon about ¼ cup of cake batter into each muffin cup and top with a peanut butter ball. Divide the remaining batter evenly among the cups to cover the peanut butter balls completely.

5. Arrange the cups on one air fryer rack and put the rack on the lower slots. Bake for 10 to 13 minutes, or until the cupcake tops look dry and set.

6. Let the cupcakes cool for about 10 minutes on a wire rack, then serve warm.

# Ingredient Cook Times Cheat Sheet

This is a general chart for reference. Your air fryer may have different cooking times and temperatures; follow the instructions that came with your appliance. Always cook foods, especially meats, poultry, and seafood, until done to a safe internal temperature. If you are using the rotisserie basket to cook these foods, no tossing or stirring is needed.

| INGREDIENT | QUANTITY | TEMPERATURE | TIME | NOTES |
|---|---|---|---|---|
| French fries (thin, frozen) | 2 to 5 cups | 390°F | 10 to 15 minutes | Remove any ice on the fries; toss or stir once during cooking. |
| French fries (thin, fresh) | 2 to 5 cups | 400°F | 15 to 20 minutes | Pat dry, toss with cornstarch and ½ teaspoon sugar for better browning, then mist with oil; toss or stir once during cooking. |
| French fries (thick, frozen) | 2 to 5 cups | 380°F | 12 to 20 minutes | Remove any ice on the fries. |
| French fries (thick, fresh) | 2 to 5 cups | 400°F | 15 to 25 minutes | Lightly spray with oil. |
| Chips | 3 to 8 cups | 400°F | 7 to 12 minutes | Toss or stir once or twice during cooking. |
| Chopped potatoes | 4 to 7 cups | 400°F | 13 to 19 minutes | Spray with oil; toss or stir once or twice during cooking. |
| Potato slices | 4 to 6 cups | 380°F | 10 to 15 minutes | Slice about ⅛ inch thick; toss with oil; toss or stir once or twice during cooking. |

| INGREDIENT | QUANTITY | TEMPERATURE | TIME | NOTES |
|---|---|---|---|---|
| Potato wedges | 2 to 5 cups | 390°F | 18 to 22 minutes | Lightly spray with oil; sprinkle with salt and pepper. |
| Cauliflower florets | 2 to 5 cups | 390°F | 5 to 9 minutes | Mist with oil and season before cooking; toss or stir once during cooking. |
| Other vegetables | 1 to 3 pounds | 350°F | Broccoli florets: 6 to 8 minutes<br><br>Green beans: whole for 6 to 7 minutes<br><br>Onions: 4 to 7 minutes<br><br>Sliced eggplant: 15 to 20 minutes<br><br>Tomatoes: whole for 8 minutes; slices for 4 minutes<br><br>Zucchini: 10 minutes | Cook vegetables individually; sliced onions work better than chopped. Cut to similar sizes. Toss or stir once during cooking. |
| Chicken breast | 2 to 6 (6-ounce) boneless, skinless halves | 360°F | 10 to 16 minutes | Cook to 165°F. Place in a single layer on the racks or baking sheets. |
| Chicken drumsticks | 2 to 6 drumsticks | 400°F and 320°F | 8 minutes at 400°F, then 10 to 12 minutes at 320°F | Pat dry; do not rinse. Spray with oil and sprinkle with seasonings. |
| Chicken nuggets | 1 to 5 cups | 370°F | 7 to 12 minutes | Remove any ice on the chicken. |

| INGREDIENT | QUANTITY | TEMPERATURE | TIME | NOTES |
|---|---|---|---|---|
| Chicken wings | 1 to 3 pounds | 380°F | 15 to 20 minutes | Cook to an internal temperature of 165°F; toss or stir once during cooking. |
| Pork chops | 1 to 4 (1-inch-thick) chops | 350°F | 7 to 10 minutes | Cook to a minimum internal temperature of 145°F. Place in a single layer on a rack or cookie sheet. |
| Burgers | 2 to 4 (4-ounce) patties | 360°F Bake 400°F Broil | 9 to 13 minutes for bake 10 to 15 minutes for broil | Place in a single layer; turn once during cooking. Cook to a minimum temperature of 160°F. |
| Meatballs (frozen) | 25 per batch | 380°F | 6 to 8 minutes | Remove any ice on the meatballs. |
| Meatballs (raw) | 25 per batch | 390°F | 6 to 10 minutes | Don't crowd; place in a single layer on a baking sheet. Turn with tongs halfway through cooking; cook to 160°F. |
| Steak | 1 to 4 (¾- to 1-inch-thick) steaks | 360°F | 8 to 11 minutes | Time depends on desired doneness; use a food thermometer to check doneness: 140°F for medium-rare, 150°F for medium. |
| Fish sticks (frozen) | 1 to 4 cups | 390°F | 8 to 10 minutes | Remove any ice on the fish. |

| INGREDIENT | QUANTITY | TEMPERATURE | TIME | NOTES |
|---|---|---|---|---|
| Shrimp (frozen) | 1 to 2 pounds | 390°F | 8 minutes | Remove any ice on the shrimp. Cooking time depends on size; larger shrimp will cook longer. |
| Shrimp (fresh) | 1 to 2 pounds | 390°F | 5 minutes | Shell and devein shrimp, pat dry. Bread before cooking (optional). |
| Salmon fillets | 4 to 6 (6-ounce) fillets | 300°F | 9 to 14 minutes | Brush with oil and sprinkle with seasonings before cooking to an internal temperature of at least 140°F. |
| Salmon steak | 4 (8-ounce) steaks | 300°F | 14 to 18 minutes | Brush with oil and sprinkle with seasonings; cook to an internal tempera-ture of at least 140°F. |
| Egg rolls | 6 to 12 | 390°F | 3 to 7 minutes | Brush or mist with oil before cooking. |
| Pizza | 1 pizza | 390°F | 5 to 11 minutes | Place pizza on parchment paper or baking sheet. Make sure it fits into the air fryer. |
| Grilled cheese sandwiches | 1 to 4 sandwiches | 400°F | 7 to 9 minutes | Place on parchment paper or a baking sheet; turn with spatula halfway through cooking. |

| INGREDIENT | QUANTITY | TEMPERATURE | TIME | NOTES |
|---|---|---|---|---|
| Cake | 1 (7- or 8-inch) pan | 320°F | 20 to 25 minutes | Bake until cake springs back when lightly touched with finger; make sure pan fits into air fryer. |
| Muffins | 6 to 8 muffins | 360°F | 10 to 12 minutes | Muffins can be baked in a muffin tin that will fit into the air fryer or doubled foil cups. |
| Fruit | 2 to 5 cups | 320°F | 3 to 5 minutes for soft fruits; 6 to 10 minutes for firm fruits | Cook hard fruits, such as apples, and soft fruits, such as peaches, separately. |

# Measurement Conversions

## Volume Equivalents (Liquid)

| US STANDARD | US STANDARD (OUNCES) | METRIC (APPROX.) |
|---|---|---|
| 2 tablespoons | 1 fl. oz. | 30 mL |
| ¼ cup | 2 fl. oz. | 60 mL |
| ½ cup | 4 fl. oz. | 120 mL |
| 1 cup | 8 fl. oz. | 240 mL |
| 1½ cups | 12 fl. oz. | 355 mL |
| 2 cups or 1 pint | 16 fl. oz. | 475 mL |
| 4 cups or 1 quart | 32 fl. oz. | 1 L |
| 1 gallon | 128 fl. oz. | 4 L |

## Oven Temperatures

| FAHRENHEIT (F) | CELSIUS (C) (APPROX.) |
|---|---|
| 250° | 120° |
| 300° | 150° |
| 325° | 165° |
| 350° | 180° |
| 375° | 190° |
| 400° | 200° |
| 425° | 220° |
| 450° | 230° |

## Volume Equivalents (Dry)

| US STANDARD | METRIC (APPROX.) |
|---|---|
| ⅛ teaspoon | 0.5 mL |
| ¼ teaspoon | 1 mL |
| ½ teaspoon | 2 mL |
| ¾ teaspoon | 4 mL |
| 1 teaspoon | 5 mL |
| 1 tablespoon | 15 mL |
| ¼ cup | 59 mL |
| ⅓ cup | 79 mL |
| ½ cup | 118 mL |
| ⅔ cup | 156 mL |
| ¾ cup | 177 mL |
| 1 cup | 235 mL |
| 2 cups or 1 pint | 475 mL |
| 3 cups | 700 mL |
| 4 cups or 1 quart | 1 L |

## Weight Equivalents

| US STANDARD | METRIC (APPROX.) |
|---|---|
| ½ ounce | 15 g |
| 1 ounce | 30 g |
| 2 ounces | 60 g |
| 4 ounces | 115 g |
| 8 ounces | 225 g |
| 12 ounces | 340 g |
| 16 ounces or 1 pound | 455 g |

# Index

# About the Author

**Linda Larsen** is an author and home economist who has been developing recipes for years. As the author of the "Busy Cooks" site for About.com for 15 years, she wrote about food safety and quick cooking. Larsen is the editor of *Food Poisoning Bulletin,* a Google news site. She has written 53 cookbooks, including *The Complete Air Fryer Cookbook, The Complete Slow Cooking for Two,* and *Eating Clean for Dummies.* Larsen has worked for the Pillsbury company since 1988, working on the Pillsbury Bake-Off and other contests. She holds a bachelor of arts degree in biology from St. Olaf College and a bachelor of science degree with high distinction in food science from the University of Minnesota. Larsen lives in Minnesota with her husband.

CPSIA information can be obtained
at www.ICGtesting.com
Printed in the USA
JSHW010912161122
33229JS00004B/6